D1595580

Plotting America's Past

FENIMORE COOPER
AND THE
LEATHERSTOCKING TALES

William P. Kelly

• Southern Illinois University Press
Carbondale and Edwardsville

For My Families

LIBRARY OF CONGRESS CATALOGING IN PUBLICATION DATA

Kelly, William P.
  Plotting America's past.

  Includes index.
    1. Cooper, James Fenimore, 1789–1851. Leatherstocking
tales. 2. Cooper, James Fenimore, 1789–1851—Knowledge—
History. 3. Historical fiction, American. 4. United
States in literature. 5. United States—Historiography.
I. Title.
PS1442.H5K44   1983   813'.2   83–4779
ISBN 0–8093–1144–5

Frontispiece is an illustration by F. O. C. Darley from *The Pathfinder*,
Townsend-Stringer edition (1859–61).

Contents

Preface

FOR one hundred and fifty years, the Leatherstocking Tales have been a point of cultural reference and a source of national identity. The decline in their readership has in no way eroded their resonance. Like the Declaration of Independence, the Gettysburg Address, *Moby-Dick*, and *Huckleberry Finn*, they have attained an extratextual status—independent of the life-support systems of the academy—and have become part of our American legacy.

Literary critics and cultural historians have both recognized and augmented the iconographic character of the Tales by describing the series as the repository of a national mythos. Natty's flight from civilization and his bond with the pristine wilderness are emblematic, we have repeatedly been told, of the Adamic longing which distinguishes and informs our cultural perspective. This emphasis addresses a significant aspect of the saga's continuing appeal, but it has had the effect of further denaturing the Tales. By converting five historical novels into a single myth, we have reduced the complexity of Cooper's vision and emptied the Tales of much of their content. This reshaping of the series is particularly ironic, because the tales represent Cooper's ardent attempt to conceptualize rather than to transcend America's history. Across the five volumes of the series, Cooper addresses his culture's relation to the past and struggles to achieve a coherent sense of historical form.

That effort is marked both by a desire for autonomy and a yearning for context. Certainly, the historiographic paradigm Cooper constructs and continually revises in the Tales suggests his attraction to flight from temporal restriction. The prospect of national primacy had for Cooper, as it did for his contemporaries, an irresistible appeal. But Cooper's repudiation of historical entailment in the Leatherstocking Tales is counterbalanced by a simultaneous defense of historical continuity. Cultural autonomy, he recognized, implied a vertiginous freedom and a precarious future. Wary of both radical originality and subservient dependence, Cooper begins the Tales by depicting America as both free from and bound to the past. In *The Pioneers* and *The Last of the Mohicans*, he is able to sustain that contradictory perspective by offering an illusory synthesis that purports to reconcile freedom and restraint.

His double vision in these novels illuminates the complexity of his culture's response to the burden of the past; but of greater interest is Cooper's subsequent reformulation of that paradigm. As the series progresses, he comes to recognize the logical inconsistencies inherent in his initial conception of America's growth and reshapes his historiographic and narrative strategies.

Contrary to a long-standing critical assumption, the thrust of that development does not carry Cooper toward a mythic discourse but leads him away from the wistful dual vision of the initial volumes of the series. In *The Deerslayer* (1841), the last of the Leatherstocking Tales, Cooper abandons the reassuring contrivances of those novels and confronts instead the limits of history. It is my primary purpose in tracing the evolution of Cooper's perspective to free the Tales from the restrictions of a mythic reading and to restore their historiographic dimension.

I would like to acknowledge the many contributions my teachers and colleagues have made to this study. William Howarth, who first encouraged my interest in American literature, has been an unflagging source of example and encouragement. Terence Martin and Lewis Miller helped me to conceptualize the project; Scott Sanders's wise counsel has been of invaluable assistance. My colleagues at Queens College—especially Frederick Buell, Jacqueline Costello, Lois Hughson, Bridget and Robert Lyons, Catherine McKenna, Donald McQuade, David Richter, Donald Stone, Michael Timko, Amy Tucker, Dennis Turner, and Ruth Vande Kieft—have been insightful readers and unfailing friends. James Pickering read my manuscript and offered many useful suggestions. Daniel Peck challenged me to rethink and expand the scope of my work. His intelligence and generosity have been a constant inspiration. I would also like to thank the other Cooper scholars whose writing has significantly informed my own. I have profited, in particular, from the scholarship of James Franklin Beard, R. W. B. Lewis, John P. McWilliams, Thomas Philbrick, Joel Porte, Stephen Railton, Donald Ringe, Richard Slotkin, Henry Nash Smith, and Eric J. Sundquist.

More personal thanks are due to Laura Wadenpfuhl, who devoted many hours to the preparation of my manuscript, to Kenney Withers, the most patient of editors, to Teresa White, who saw the book through to completion, and to Arnold Auerbach, who helped preserve my spirits. Finally, I am grateful for the support of my parents, the understanding of my wife, Sarah, and the good cheer of my daughter, Ann. Thanks to each and all.

Plotting America's Past

❦ I ❧

The Pioneers
and the
Abridgements of History
❦❧

Insist on yourself; never imitate.

—*Emerson*, Self-Reliance

Our debt to tradition through reading and conversation is so massive, our protest or private addition so rare and insignificant— and this commonly on the ground of other reading or hearing— that, in a large sense, one would say there is no pure originality. All minds quote. Old and new make the warp and woof of every moment. There is no thread that is not a twist of these two strands. By necessity, by proclivity and by delight, we all quote.

—*Emerson*, Quotation and
Originality

The difficulty is that we do not make a world of our own but fall into institutions already made and have to accommodate our- selves to them to be useful at all. And this accommodation, is, I say, a loss, of so much integrity and, of course, of so much power. But how shall the droning world get on if all its beaux espirits recalcitrate upon its approved forms and accepted institutions and quit them in order to be single minded? The double refiners would produce at the other end the double damned.

—*Emerson*, Blotting Book

TEMPLETON, the frontier village in which Fenimore Cooper sets *The Pioneers* (1823), is a community poised between order and chaos. Throughout the early years of

its history, civil authority has been lodged in the hands of
Judge Marmaduke Temple, the settlement's founder.
Temple has, without challenge, cleared the wilderness,
fostered the development of commerce and agriculture,
and established a rudimentary system of government. But
as the novel opens, the Judge begins to encounter the first
stirrings of resistance. His settlers, whose prosperity is
now secure, have become restive under his paternal rule.
They regard his laws as unwarranted infringements on
their liberty and reject his efforts to limit their exploitation
of the forests. Their mounting antagonism is paralleled by
the opposition of three characters who are victims of the
historical process which has yielded Templeton. Chingachgook, the last survivor of the Mohican tribe which original-
ly held Temple's land; Natty Bumppo, an aged hunter
whose tenure in the area far exceeds that of the settlers; and
Oliver Effingham, the heir of the British family whose
forfeited patent the Judge has acquired, have each been
displaced by the progress Temple has sponsored. Living as
a family on the fringe of the village, they dispute the legitimacy of the Judge's power.[1]

In the concluding chapters of *The Pioneers*, Cooper defuses both of these threats to civil order. Temple has not,
Oliver Effiingham discovers, cheated his father, the Judge's
patron and former partner. Rather, Oliver's father's obstinancy and a series of unopened letters have led Temple
to believe that Oliver is dead and that the Effingham line
has been extinguished. When Oliver at last reveals his
identity, the Judge immediately rectifies that misunder-

---

1 See Thomas Philbrick's discussion of *The Pioneers'* movement from
"suppressed enmity to the verge of violence" in "Cooper's *The Pioneers*:
Origins and Structure," *PMLA* 79 (December 1964): 579–93.

standing and restores his inheritance. In the novel's final chapter, Oliver seals their reconciliation by marrying Temple's daughter, Elizabeth, and receives the Judge's assurance that he will succeed him as the proprietor of his Templeton holdings.

The claims of Natty Bumppo and Chingachgook are similarly dispatched. They have advanced their territorial prerogatives, Natty ultimately explains, not on their own behalf but on Oliver's. Chingachgook's tribe had deeded the land on which Templeton now stands to Oliver's grandfather, Major Effingham, in whose service Natty was employed. Natty and Chingachgook have remained in Templeton, we learn, to preserve the family's interests, and with Oliver's marriage, they resign their quarrel with Judge Temple. Cooper discharges their disruptive force as fully as he resolves Oliver's dispute with the Judge. Chingachgook dies, rendering moot the issue of Indian rights. Relieved of his duty to Major Effingham, Natty gives his blessing to Oliver and Elizabeth and departs for the wilderness to conclude his life in peace.

Cooper also firmly checks the discontent of Templeton's settlers. Their conflict with the Judge reaches its climax when they falsely accuse Natty and Oliver of starting a forest fire which threatens the village. Banding together "in [a] feverish state," the community becomes a mob intent on revenge.[2] Just as the anarchy and violence, which is implicit throughout *The Pioneers*, is about to erupt, Temple appears and demands that the angry crowd disperse. "Silence and peace!" he orders, "why do I see

<hr/>

2 James Fenimore Cooper, *The Pioneers* (Albany, N.Y., 1980), 426. Future references will be to this edition and will be cited by page number in the text.

murder and bloodshed attempted! is not the law sufficient
to protect itself, that armed bands must be gathered, as in
rebellion or war, to see justice performed!" (435). For
the first time in the novel, Temple's power is fully acknowledged. The chastened citizens submit to his authority and
return to their homes. Cooper then affirms the lasting effect
of the Judge's intervention by remarking that "the growing
wealth and intelligence" of the village's residents soon
rendered them more law-abiding and less susceptible to the
restless impulses of frontier democracy (446).

The Pioneers' progress from discord to harmony is not,
of course, an indication of Cooper's originality. A final assembling of characters, the revelation of previously con-
cealed secrets, and the disposition of narrative tensions is a
trope as old as fiction itself. Indeed, both of Cooper's prior
novels, *Precaution* (1820) and *The Spy* (1821), build to
similar resolutions of opposing viewpoints. There is, however, a significant aspect of *The Pioneers'* denouement
which distinguishes this novel from its generic models and
from Cooper's earlier work. The closure Cooper effects
here is not directed primarily toward the abatement of the
private conflicts of his characters or the social pressures of
the frontier but toward the creation of historical form.

Cooper declares his historiographic intentions in the
opening paragraphs of *The Pioneers*. There he contrasts
the contemporary condition of the novel's setting with its
primitive origins. "Beautiful and thriving villages," he
writes,

> are found interspersed along the margins of the small lakes,
> or situated at those points of the streams which are favourable
> to manufacturing; and neat and comfortable farms, with every
> indication of wealth about them, are scattered profusely through

the vales, and even to the mountain tops. Roads diverge in every direction, from the even and graceful bottoms of the valleys, to the most rugged and intricate passes of the hills. Academies, and minor edifices of learning, meet the eye of the stranger, at every few miles, as he winds his way through this uneven territory; and places for the worship of God abound with that frequency which characterizes a moral and reflecting people, and with that variety of exterior and canonical government which flows from unfettered liberty of conscience.

This pastoral condition, Cooper maintains, is the product of a continuing social evolution:

The whole district is hourly exhibiting how much can be done, in even a rugged country, and with a severe climate, under the dominion of mild laws, and where every man feels a direct interest in the prosperity of a commonwealth, of which he knows himself to form a part. The expedients of the pioneers who first broke ground in the settlement of this country, are succeeded by the permanent improvements of the yeoman, who intends to leave his remains to moulder under the sod which he tills, or, perhaps, of the son, who, born in the land, piously wishes to linger around the grave of his father. Only forty years have passed since this whole territory was a wilderness.

Having established the virtues of present-day New York, Cooper announces that his novel will focus on the initial stage of settlement in the area—the period that has generated "the beautiful and thriving villages" he has described. "Our tale," he concludes, "begins in 1793, about seven years after the commencement of one of the earliest of those settlements, which have conduced to effect that magical change in the power and condition of the state, to which we have alluded" (15–16).

By beginning *The Pioneers* with this historical overview, Cooper anticipates his conclusion and undermines whatever suspense the novel might produce. *Whether* a given set of conflicts will be eased is not at issue in *The Pioneers*. Rather, we are called upon to question *how* its resolutions have prepared the way for the tranquility of contemporary New York. The interest of the novel, we are told immediately, is causality—the dynamics of American development. The challenges to Judge Temple's authority, which shape Cooper's narrative, most certainly address issues of social and individual principle, but these concerns are subsumed by Cooper's efforts to designate the shaping forces responsible for "the magical change" he perceives in forty years of national history.

The rivalry Cooper forges between Judge Temple and Oliver Effingham is, for example, not simply a reworking of the missing heir motif so common in protoromantic fiction but is a restaging of the tensions inherent in America's revolutionary origins. Temple's break with Oliver's father, Colonel Effingham, was provoked, Cooper explains, by their divergent loyalties. Effingham's decision to defend the royalist cause has resulted in the loss of his colonial holdings; Temple's patriotism has, in turn, permitted him to purchase Effingham's lands and launch his settlement. Oliver's marriage to Elizabeth Temple obviously suggests the reunification of America in the postwar period of the novel's setting, but more important than the fact of national reconciliation—which Oliver's ascendancy records—is Cooper's description of that process in dialectical terms. The grandson of Major Effingham, the colonial proprietor of Temple's estate, Oliver embodies the refinement of British culture. He is, at the same time, the figurative son of Natty and Chingachgook, with whom he lives in the novel's opening chapters. Distant from the crudity of Judge

Temple's village and the narrow vision of the Old World, he unifies the grace of Europe, the self-discipline of Indian life, and the forest-taming energies of young America. His marriage not only terminates a familial and a national feud but also epitomizes, for Cooper, the characteristic thrust of American history.

Cooper's ordering of the novel's other conflicts reenforces this definition of historical form. Judge Temple duplicates Oliver Effingham's function by resisting both the settler's demands for unlimited expansion and Natty and Chingachgook's insistence that all progress cease. Incorporating a respect for nature with a commitment to western development, he creates in Templeton a middle ground equally distant from a European city and a trackless wilderness. Just as Temple's ability to reconcile conflicting polarities anticipates the more refined mediation of Oliver Effingham, Natty's role foreshadows that of the Judge. A white man who has internalized the precepts of Indian culture, he stands between Temple and the original inhabitants of the forest. His antisocial temperament and his celibacy limit his status to that of a precursor, but the cultural synthesis he achieves inaugurates the historical process which Temple extends and Effingham completes.

Further examples of the dialectical syntax of *The Pioneers* are easily marshaled. The civil law which Judge Temple introduces balances Natty's internal discipline and the anarchic impulses of the settlers. A religious conflict in the village between the adherents of Anglican orthodoxy and those of evangelical Methodism is mediated by the rational Christianity of the Reverend Grant. The multinational residents of Templeton abandon their hereditary grievances to become Americans. The winter and summer settings of the novel's major events yield in *The Pioneers'* final chapter to "the delightful month of October" in which "the weather [is] neither too warm, nor too cold, but of that happy temperature which stirs the blood, without bringing the lassitude of spring" (447). Judge Temple secures his rapprochement with Oliver Effingham and affirms the wisdom of moderation by arguing that in the past "we have both erred; thou hast been too hasty, and I have been too slow" (443).

In stressing the dialectical character of *The Pioneers'* narrative strategy, I am not attempting merely to establish Cooper's world view as one which privileges balance and moderation. Certainly those values occupied a central place in Cooper's mental landscape. He was an heir of the American Enlightenment and remained throughout his life a subscriber to the tenets of that ideology. But more interesting than the presence of those eighteenth-century assumptions in the novel is the use to which they are directed. In *The Pioneers*, Cooper's affirmation of Enlightenment ideals not only serves a didactic purpose but also becomes the basis of his historiographic strategy.

I hasten to clarify that distinction. In *Precaution* and *The Spy*, Cooper defends the same moderate principles he invokes in *The Pioneers*. The matrimonial crises of *Precaution* demonstrate the need for a heightened level of personal and familial responsibility. Cooper contrasts the excessive freedom the Moseley's grant their daughter Jane with the more balanced guidance Mrs. Wilson offers Jane's sister Emily. By encouraging Emily's independence, while she simultaneously nurtures the growth of her self-discipline, Mrs. Wilson prepares Emily for a successful marriage. Jane's embarrassment when her unworthy suitor, Colonel Egerton, jilts her for an heiress documents the wisdom of Emily's discretion and secures Cooper's moral lesson. Social order, he argues, demands the adoption of rational restraints and the suppression of unlicensed freedom.

Although *The Spy* is ostensibly more historical in character than *Precaution*, Cooper is, in his second novel, less interested in charting the direction of American time than he is in establishing standards to guide the nation's destiny. The revolutionary war is not an initiating event in *The Spy* but a backdrop against which Cooper sets the familiar Enlightenment conflict between reason and fanaticism. Condemning expediency in both the Tory and the Patriot camps, Cooper employs the past as a storehouse of example capable of inculcating sound judgment in the present. Like *Precaution*, *The Spy* is a moral tract which imposes a social vision on its readers. The declaration of universal principles of conduct and not the investigation of an historical trajectory is its overriding objective.

Cooper does not entirely abandon his didactic intentions in *The Pioneers*, but he does subordinate them to more genuinely historiographic concerns. The resolutions he crafts in his concluding chapters, as well as the subsidiary mediations he effects throughout his narrative, do suggest a standard of conduct. Concurrently, however, they define a temporal process. America begins with Natty Bumppo's synthesis of European and Indian values, it advances as Judge Temple orders the contending claims of progress and stasis, and it reaches its telos in Oliver Effingham's reconciliation of the constituent traditions of American life.

Moderation and compromise, in short, cease in *The Pioneers* to be values a culture should aspire toward and become the mechanisms that have given that culture shape and direction.

This transition from the didacticism of *Precaution* and *The Spy* to the historicism of *The Pioneers* is a crucial one for Cooper's development as an artist. In his first two novels, Cooper predicated his fiction on questions of personal responsibility. The world at large was only an arena in which moral postures were tested and a particular value system affirmed. In *The Pioneers* Cooper relocates his characters within a historical frame and employs their conflicts to identify the determining force of American development. Although he does not suspend free will in *The Pioneers*, Cooper suggests that individual choice is significant only to the degree that it advances or retards the inexorble march of time. As Cooper's focus expands so too does the resonance of his fiction. The commonplace defense of Enlightenment values which marks *Precaution* and *The Spy* yields to a complex engagement of the broad web of shared concerns within which human destinies are transacted.

The historiographic interests of *The Pioneers* also establish Cooper's centrality as an American writer. Cultural historians have frequently overstated the extent of social flux during the 1820s, but the generation that came of age during that decade did confront a crisis of cultural definition. America's boundaries were expanding at a rapid rate, and although the settlement of new territories was an occasion for national pride, that growth also suggested the prospect of cultural diffusion. From the initial moments of the colonial period, the frontier had been associated in the

American mind with the erosion of civil authority.[3] The unprecedented scope of western movement in the years following the War of 1812 exacerbated that concern in a concrete way. The mounting population and power of the New West ruptured traditional economic and regional coalitions and forced the nation to reconsider its priorities. The political perspectives which had shaped American vision since the time of the Revolution were inadequate to defuse the impact of this challenge to the status quo. In the face of national expansion and the extension of suffrage, the Federalist hegemony dissipated its energies in a futile defense of regional and class privilege. Simultaneously, Republican leadership fragmented under the weight of increasing pluralism. Whig and Democratic efforts to reformulate political thought in response to a changing America were as yet largely incoherent.

In growing numbers, Americans reacted to this shifting national fabric by turning to the past. Interest in the nation's history, which had begun to build at the turn of the century, reached a new peak in the 1820s and 1830s. A plethora of local histories, memoirs, and biographies appeared; antiquarian and historical societies were chartered; historical fiction gained a new popularity. Cooper's efforts to engage the American past in *The Pioneers* reflects this broadly shared sensibility; but his novel is not just a barometer of its times. It is a work which organizes and extends that structure of feeling. More comprehensive and coherent

3 For discussions of the anarchic implications of the frontier see Edwin Fussell, *Frontier: American Literature and the American West* (Princeton, 1965); Richard Slotkin, *Regeneration through Violence: The Mythology of the American Frontier, 1600–1860* (Middletown, Conn., 1973); and Henry Nash Smith, *Virgin Land: The American West as Symbol and Myth* (New York, 1950).

than any historiographic text of its period, *The Pioneers*
identifies and allays contemporary anxiety by containing
an uncertain future within a fixed temporal process.

In advancing a claim for *The Pioneers'* cultural centrality, I do not mean to suggest that either *Precaution* or
The Spy is divorced from its social context. *Precaution*'s
dependence on British literary and social models signals
the absence of a national tradition in the early nineteenth-
century; *The Spy*'s tentative exploration of the American
past gives voice to a developing nationalism which was to
climax in the major works of the American renaissance.
Moreover, the intellectual assumptions of both of these
novels—their defense of Enlightenment values—clearly
establish their representative status. The imagination op-
erating in *The Pioneers* is, however, of a different order.
Rather than simply evoking the temper of his times, Cooper advances a solution to the culturally bound problem
he identifies. By deriving order from the flux of historical
events, he redefines the present and the future as the products
of a system of causality. Within Cooper's paradigm, design replaces chaos and ordered development becomes a
certainty.

And yet, *The Pioneers'* significance does not reside
primarily in Cooper's attempt to defuse contemporary un-
certainty about the future. More important are the contradictions Cooper blurs in realizing the comforting perspective he offers his readers. Despite the rigorous closure
Cooper imposes on his narrative conflicts, the reconciliations
he crafts and the historical perspective he advances remain
unpersuasive. The calm which prevails in the novel's final
chapters is too easily won; the tensions Cooper engages are
repressed rather than resolved. Although Cooper's historio-

graphic thesis is coherent and precise, the logic he employs to defend it does not bear close scrutiny. There is a contrived quality about *The Pioneers'* conclusion which makes its silences and deletions more compelling than its confident projection of American progress.

These inconsistencies, which I will discuss at some length, do not proceed from Cooper's inadequacies as a writer but stem from the complexity of the historiographic problem he addresses in *The Pioneers*. Cooper's intentions are largely conservative. In the midst of disconcerting social flux, he turns to the past to reduce the anxieties occasioned by a problematic future. By establishing a coherent pattern of American development—a dynamic that transcends individual action—Cooper attempts to guarantee national security. His version of the course of American history implies, however, an admission of entailment and a denial of originality. Within the temporal frame Cooper constructs in *The Pioneers*, derivation is inevitable. The present and the future at best only extend a series of dialectical mediations established in the past. Natty Bumppo's synthesis of Indian and European culture depends upon the centuries of Old World progress that led to American settlement. Judge Temple and Oliver Effingham, in turn, refine the mediation Natty achieves. Although this assumption of forced continuity alleviated one cultural concern, it activated another. The price of the social stability Cooper's historiographic model affirmed was a denial of primacy, a recognition of the burden of the past.

Such an admission was, of course, in conflict with the Adamic presumption at the heart of American belief. To accept the determining role of history was to surrender autonomy, self-reliance, and the eternal prospect of new

beginnings. While such a resignation of the very props of
national identity would be unthinkable at any period of
cultural history, an admission of historical dependence was
particularly difficult for Cooper's generation. Both the cultural imperialism of Europe and the towering achievements
of the founding fathers severely circumscribed the range
of potential achievement available to Americans in the
1820s. Cooper's contemporaries, who were well aware of
this constraining context, were predisposed to interpret
history in a manner consistent with their desire to repudiate
a debilitating anxiety of cultural and generational influence.[4]

In plotting the form of American time in *The Pioneers*,
then, Cooper confronted diametrically opposed imperatives. The precarious nature of the status quo—imperiled
by the proximity of the frontier and the disruption of
traditional patterns of social and political organization—
led him toward a defense of historical continuity. By conceptualizing American experience as a mechanical process
governed by fixed principles of development, he could
effectively respond to contemporary concern about the nation's future. But as a member of a postrevolutionary generation informed by both a self-reliant ethos and a longing
for historical liberation, Cooper was drawn to deny the
determining power of the European and American past.
His efforts to establish a historical frame were, therefore,
complicated by a double vision. A commitment to design
a controlling temporal order co-existed with an urge to

---

4 The most comprehensive survey of America's flight from inscription
remains R. W. B. Lewis's *The American Adam: Innocence, Tragedy, and
Tradition in the Nineteenth Century* (Chicago, 1955), but see also Eric J.
Sundquist's brilliant analysis of generational anxiety in *Home as Found:
Authority and Genealogy in Nineteenth-Century American Literature* (Balti-
more, 1979).

displace historical paternity. In *The Pioneers* Cooper does not acknowledge the mutually exclusive nature of these competing demands but consistently blurs their contradiction. The central thrust of his narrative is toward the creation of a historical paradigm which imposes meaning and direction on national experience. But in crafting that model, Cooper qualifies repeatedly his assertions of temporal entailment. Struggling to establish a perspective which embraces both difference and repetition, he argues that the America of 1823 is both free from, and bound to, the past.

The most obvious example of Cooper's conflicting intentions is his characterization of Judge Temple. A model of paternal strength, the Judge has fostered settlement in the wilderness, provided for his people during times of scarcity, ruled with wisdom and restraint, and secured the prosperity of his descendants. If on occasion, his ambition appears excessive, it is the well-being of the community and not self-interest that he pursues. Cooper consistently establishes Temple's personal merits as a standard of context, discipline, and rational growth. His role, as Cooper defines it, is not only that of a frontier patriarch but that of a cultural polestar. By coupling, for example, a discussion of Judge Temple's game laws with reports of revolutionary excess in France, Cooper makes explicit Temple's metaphoric status. In checking the nascent anarchy of Templeton, he secures the promise of America's future.

Cooper qualifies, however, the monumental scale his narrative accords Judge Temple. Although he emphasizes Temple's commitment to restore the Effingham lands, he does juxtapose Colonel Effingham's selfless loyalism with the Judge's more pragmatic patriotism. Cooper tells us that the Judge assisted colonial forces "in various civil capacities, and always with dignity and usefulness," but he observes that, unlike Effingham, he "never seemed to lose sight of his own interests." His cautious regard for his own advancement has enabled him, for example, to purchase "at, comparatively, low prices" the confiscated Effingham estate (36).[5] Temple's opportunism has "rendered him obnoxious to the censures" of his peers, but "his success, or the frequency of the transgression in others, soon wiped this slight stain from his character" (36). Cooper's posture parallels the response of the Judge's neighbors. He, too, subordinates Temple's initial shrewdness to his subsequent achievements and honorable intentions, but like the citizens of Templeton who whisper "dark hints concerning the sudden prosperity of the unportioned quaker," Cooper never entirely acquits the Judge of the suspicions that cloud his origins (37).

Cooper further subverts Temple's stature by involving him in a number of compromising episodes. None of these incidents is significant in itself—and indeed Cooper consistently offsets the Judge's weakness with examples of his strength—but taken together they effectively erode Temple's moral authority. In the opening scene of the novel, the Judge fires a fowling piece at a buck that crosses the path of his sleigh. Temple's discharge has no effect, but two other shots that follow closely on his own kill the fleeing deer. When Natty and Oliver Effingham, who have fired the successful shots, appear from the cover of the forest to claim their prize, Temple disputes their possession by maintaining, against clear evidence to the contrary, that his

5 See Andrew Nelson's discussion of William Cooper's acquisition of his Lake Otsego holdings in "James Cooper and George Croghan," *Philological Quarterly* 20 (1941): 69–73.

weapon struck the deer first and that their shots were acts
of "supererogation" (23). When Natty resists the Judge's
duplicit efforts to deprive him of his kill, Temple resorts
to bribery. "Sell me the venison," he tells Natty and Effingham, "and the deuce is in it, but I make a good story about
its death" (24). It is, the Judge admits, "for the honour
that I contend," an honor he would purchase without merit
or shame (22).

Cooper retreats from his attack on the Judge's hypocrisy by redirecting his readers' attention to Temple's benev-
olence. One of his bullets has wounded Effingham and
when the Judge discovers his injury, he immediately regrets
"trifling here about an empty distinction" and offers Effingham both medical aid and a lifetime residence in his
home (24). His generosity does not, however, entirely
obscure his expediency. Like the scattered shot of his fowling piece Temple's principles lack precision. Neither Effingham's wound nor the Judge's attempted bribery has serious
consequences, but they do suggest a disturbing precedent.
The Judge's weapon "don't do," Natty tells him, "to hunt
in company with" (27). Nor will his unfocused morality
"do," Cooper implies, as a standard of social authority.

Cooper reenforces this initial incident with additional
examples of Temple's flexible morality. Although he is no
longer a practicing Quaker, he pays lip service to his sect's
abolitionist principles. But when he requires a servant for
his home, he evades that sanction by purchasing a slave in
the name of his cousin, Richard Jones. He declaims against
the settlers' wanton slaughter of game, but caught up in
the excitement of a pigeon hunt, he participates in their
wasteful sport. His subsequent repentance is doubtlessly
sincere, but it does not fully restore his stature. The Judge

argues that "living, as we do, . . . on the skirts of society,"
an absolute respect for the law and its officers must be preserved (369). When he names a sheriff for the district,
however, he chooses Jones, a man of manifestly poor judgment whose sole qualification for the post is his kinship
with Temple. Rather than preserving the community's
peace, Jones and his deputy Hiram Doolittle continually
provoke conflict and turmoil.

The crudity of Temple's community provides Cooper
with another opportunity to diminish the Judge's authority.
Temple's instructions for the building of his home have
called for the construction of a simple but dignified residence. But in executing that request, Richard Jones has
erected a "Mansion-house" that is the subject of Cooper's
sustained ridicule. Rather than supporting the roof, the
mansion's columns are suspended from it and fail by a foot
to reach the ground. In an attempt to disguise the ill-
conceived proportions of the roof itself, Jones has painted
it a "sunshine" yellow and ornamented it with "gaudily
painted railings" and "divers urns and mouldings" (44).
The mansion's entrance hall is dominated by a large stove
and an iron water basin which serves as a primitive humidi-
fier. The Judge's furnishings—most particularly a series
of blacked plaster of paris busts of Homer, Shakespeare,
Franklin, Washington, and a nondescript figure Jones
identifies as either "Julius Caesar or Dr. Faustus"—are dis-
cordant and of homely manufacture (64). His wallpaper,
which depicts Britannia weeping over the tomb of Wolfe,
has been hung in a fashion which ceaselessly amputates
Wolfe's right arm.

The manner of Temple's establishment is consistent
with its design. The Judge's table offers a "profusion . . .

obtained entirely at the expense of order and elegance"
(108). His friends eat and drink with great enthusiasm
but with little decorum. Temple's servants are clownish
figures who lack even the rudiments of domestic refinement.
His cook, Remarkable Pettibone, to whom "the idea of
being governed, or of being compelled to pay the deference
of servitude, was absolutely intolerable," insists on calling
the Judge's daughter "Lizzy" and rebels against her efforts
to bring discipline to his household (169). Ben Pump, the
mansion's steward, is a misplaced sailor whose good humor
does not disguise his incompetence. Temple's slave, Agamemnon, is a stereotypic black capable only of maudlin
sentimentality and trembling cowardice. Again, however,
Cooper moderates the severity of his criticism. By attributing the mansion's vulgarity to Jones's modification of
the Judge's plans, Cooper preserves Temple's dignity while
he parodies his home. He distances the Judge from his
guests and servants and imparts considerable charm to the
novel's social gatherings. Nevertheless, the insistent condescension of Cooper's narration reduces Temple's preeminence.

Cooper's description of Templeton is as patronizing
as his account of the Mansion-house. Huge "heaps of logs"
clog the village's streets, and blackened stumps mar the
beauty of its fields. The fifty buildings of the settlement
are grouped together, Cooper writes, "in a manner that
aped the streets of a city." Their architecture "bore no
great marks of taste," and "by the unfinished appearance
of most of the dwellings, indicated the hasty manner of
their construction." A few of the village's homes have been
adorned with white paint, but they employ "that ex-
pensive color on their fronts only." The town's window-

panes are broken; the interior design of its better homes
reflects the vanity which had led their proprietors "to un-
dertake a task which they were unable to accomplish."
Cooper extends the mock-heroic quality of his description
of Temple's Mansion-house by identifying the occupants
of "these favoured habitations" as the "nobles of Templeton" (41–42). The refinement of the settlement's residents parallels the primitive character of their village.
Their dress is eccentric; their syntax irregular. They gather
at the Bold Dragoon, a tavern, which next to the Mansion-
house, is "by far the most conspicuous edifice" in the village (145). There the community's unqualified profession-
als banter in mangled Latin, drink to excess from the same
cup, and spit freely on the floor.

Cooper's extended accounts of the town's barbarity may
be attributed to a number of factors. First, by stressing the
humble origins of Templeton and by juxtaposing that image
with his description of the "thriving villages" and "neat
and comfortable farms" of contemporary New York, Cooper validates the meliorist assumptions of his historiographic paradigm. A demonstration of progress, after all,
requires a point of departure. Second, Cooper's portrayal
of his fictional village may be explained as an effort to
achieve a picturesque quality mandated by his associationist
aesthetic. Consistent with that intention, Cooper's ridicule
is leavened with a nostalgic affection that recalls Washington Irving and early American genre painting. Third,
Cooper's account of frontier Templeton redeems his intention—announced as a subtitle—to write "a descriptive tale."
The primitive conditions he recounts are congruent with
other contemporary reports of wilderness settlement, and
in fact, Cooper's description of Templeton is less harsh

than the majority of those narratives.[6] Irrespective of these rationales, however, Cooper's belabored accounts of Templeton's failings are directed primarily toward the reduction of the intimidating stature of Judge Temple and his generation. Cooper types the Judge as a benign but unpolished "king" who occupies a drafty Mansion-house and rules a motley collection of nobles and contentious peasants. As much as he may separate Temple from the crudity of his community, Cooper distances himself and his contemporaries even further from the Judge, claiming, thereby, a primacy for his generation's refinement if not for its historical location.

But Cooper's most serious assault on Temple's stature is not directed against either his morality or his taste but against his potency. In theory, the Judge's power is absolute —he alone determines and administers the laws that govern his community. The order which prevails in the novel's conclusion must, therefore, be regarded as his accomplishment. But by ceding that triumph to the Judge, Cooper necessarily limits the range of his generation's achievement. By bringing order to the frontier, Temple has won the crucial battle for national security—contemporary America can only follow in his footsteps. Cooper responds to this entailment by undermining the Judge's role in civilizing the wilderness. Although Temple does demonstrate his authority by dispersing the villagers when they take arms against Natty and Oliver, that display of power is inconsistent with his prior performance in the novel.

6 See, e.g., descriptions of frontier villages in Hugh Henry Brackenridge's *Modern Chivalry*, Timothy Dwight's *Travels in New England and New-York*, *The Journal of Sarah Kemble Knight*, and *The Journals of Francis Parkman*. See, too, Cooper's father's account of the settlement of Cooperstown in *A Guide in the Wilderness* (Dublin, 1810).

Throughout *The Pioneers* Judge Temple opposes the rapacious energy of the settlers. He secures game laws, dispenses justice in his courtroom, and plans for the orderly expansion of the community. But these attempts to instill discipline in the village are ineffective. His demand that Templeton's sugar maples be preserved is openly flaunted in his own household. Jones freely burns maple logs while he ridicules the Judge's scruples. Temple can only "earnestly beg" the woodsman Billy Kirby to gather the maples' sap in a less destructive manner and, when Kirby scorns his request, must content himself by remarking that "opinions on such subjects vary much" (229). Temple's plans for the community's design are frustrated by the settlers' random inclinations. Their shortcuts and not his maps determine the course of the village's highways. The Judge argues passionately against the speculative transactions of the settlers, but lots and businesses continue to be exchanged on a seasonal basis. His efforts to halt the pigeon kill and bass netting that Jones organizes are futile. His insistence that such greed be checked is laudable, but as Cooper argues, Temple "appeared to understand that all opposition to the will of the Sheriff would be useless" (266). Not only in these incidents but in a number of other episodes in the novel as well, the Judge's ability to restrain his cousin is precarious at best. Jones, who despite, or perhaps because of, his aristocratic pretensions is a nightmarish emblem of leveling democracy, is less the Judge's deputy than he is his competitor.

From one perspective, then, Cooper casts Judge Temple as a symbol of order and progress whose triumph over both reaction and rebellion grounds *The Pioneers'* vision of American history. But simultaneously, Cooper limits

Temple's primacy by opening a considerable gap between the Judge's era and his own. The "magical change" Cooper perceives in national development has radically altered the setting of the novel. The primitive meeting house and stump-strewn fields of Templeton have given way to "academies of higher learning" and "the permanent improvements of the yeoman." Cooper's patronizing descriptions of Temple's impotence and of the failings of his taste and morality disqualify the Judge as the agent of that change.

It is Effingham and not Temple who emerges as the author of the present. He is Temple's heir, and the Judge has contributed to his development, but Effingham is not Temple's true son nor is he his creation. His manner is fully cultivated prior to his arrival in Templeton; the quality of his mind is alien to Temple's more primitive sensibility. Cooper does not explicitly attribute the change that has transformed frontier Templeton to Effingham's leadership, nor does he examine the years that intervene between the novel's setting and its composition. But by placing the community's destiny in Effingham's hands and by describing contemporary New York as a society consistent with his taste rather than with Temple's, Cooper implicitly affirms the centrality of Effingham's role. The novel's strategy, then, is resolutely doubled. The Judge remains a figure of paternal authority who provides a reassuring context, but the America of 1823 is not the immediate product of his labors. In rising to power, Effingham becomes both father and son. Bound to England, to colonial America, to Indian culture, and to frontier Templeton, he affirms historical continuity. Concurrently, he is a figure of departure and originality who initiates a process of social change which culminates in a new America.

The contradictory nature of Cooper's portrayal of
Judge Temple is particularly apparent in one of the rare
scenes in *The Pioneers* in which the Judge effectively ex-
ercises his authority. When Natty Bumppo kills a deer out
of season, Temple refuses to temper his justice with mercy
and sentences him to a prison term and to public humiliation in the stocks. As an abstraction, the Judge's action
demonstrates the strength of his commitment to order and
law, but his decision is complicated by the countertext of
the novel. Natty is a powerless victim whose right to hunt
in the woods is, as he argues, "of older date than Marmaduke Temple's right to forbid him" (25). In Temple's
own words he is "an exception," a man whose self-discipline
does not require the support of civil law (202). Furthermore, because he has in another episode of the novel saved
Elizabeth's life, Natty has a profound claim on Temple's
compassion. The Judge has no choice but to convict Natty.
The punishment he must inflict is, however, clearly disproportionate to his crime and poor recompense for Bumppo's service to his daughter. By making Natty the focus
of Temple's justice, Cooper reduces the Judge's character
without diminishing his support for the controlling context he represents.

Not only does this confrontation demonstrate Temple's power without redressing his impotence, but it undermines as well his position as a sympathetic figure. Rather
than a nurturing father, he becomes, in this scene at least, a
tyrant who upholds the letter of the law at the expense of
its spirit. In response to his judgment Elizabeth and Effingham are drawn together in filial revolt and help Natty to
escape from Temple's jail. It is reductive to read the
Judge's punishment of Natty either as an assault on Tem-

ple's character or as a validation of his power. It is most certainly both. Natty's conviction supports the Judge's authority in the abstract while it diminishes it in the concrete. Temple is required by his frontier circumstances to administer justice in a harsh and absolute fashion. His willingness to do so secures Cooper's historiographic model and provides him with a reassuring and instructive context. But Temple's verdict reduces his moral and social authority and provides sufficient range for future leadership which is both certain and humane.

Cooper's strategy of defending and subverting Temple's primacy—of affirming and disrupting generational continuity—is duplicated in his consideration of national identity. Effingham's marriage forwards a view of America as a synthetic culture, a product of the dialectical resolution of competing traditions. Effingham's heritage and education are English. Despite his American holdings and his honorary membership in the Mohican tribe, Oliver's grandfather, Major Effingham, remains a British loyalist. He resists real kinship with the Indians and opposes the colonial struggle for independence. Even as an impoverished old man hidden in Natty's cabin, he denies the process of change which has elevated Judge Temple to a position of power. He lives entirely in the past and insists in his confusion that "each one who loves a good and virtuous king, will wish to see these colonies continue loyal" (437). His son, Colonel Effingham, is equally inflexible. He has disguised his partnership with Temple in deference to his father's contempt for Quakers and for commerce, has opposed the American Revolution as a British officer, and has refused to open letters from Temple which would have restored his property.

At the beginning of the novel, Oliver Effingham is committed to his family's opposition to Temple. Assuming a false identity, he resists, as Oliver Edwards, the progress which Temple promotes. But through his relationships with Natty and Chingachgook, who teach him a new way of life, and with Marmaduke and Elizabeth Temple, who convince him of the injustice of his grievances, Oliver abandons the recalcitrance of his father and grandfather. In succeeding both to the Effingham claims and to the Judge's own property, he resolves three generations of conflict and brings a new legitimacy to Temple's patent. By *The Pioneers'* final chapter, all of the novel's contending parties have acknowledged him as their heir. He has, as he tells Elizabeth, "forgotten [his] name and family" to reconcile the contending heritages of the novel (412). The product of European refinement and American energy, he embodies the trajectory of American history.

As clearly as Effingham's succession demonstrates the holistic nature of history, his triumph also establishes national and generational autonomy. Cooper distances his location within the progressive continuum of the novel from that of his multiple fathers. Effingham's bonds to Natty, Chingachgook, Colonel and Major Effingham, and Judge Temple are legitimate. He does represent a stage of civilization which is nourished by the past, but the extent of his difference from these fathers suggests more than a generational transit. Natty and Chingachgook are clearly beings of another order of experience. Despite his merits, the Judge is a man of the frontier; Colonel and Major Effingham are residual elements of a colonial culture. Oliver finally shares very few of their assumptions. Cooper emphasizes his singularity through a form of temporal algebra. Five years in America, he maintains, "had wrought greater changes, than a century would produce in countries, where time and labor have given permanency to the works of man" (46). This accelerated temporal pace results in a gap of eight hundred European years between the novel's setting and its composition. Cooper is able, therefore, to maintain continuity while establishing difference. Effingham is the son of the novel's fathers, just as contemporary America is the heir of European and revolutionary history, but because time in the New World is so accelerated, paternity recedes to the point of insignificance. Effingham and the America of 1823 are not without context, but that heritage is displaced by the novel's temporal equation. Cooper has created an extensive context where none exists, thereby disarming the intrusive force of history while he preserves its comforting frame. All of Effingham's fathers become passive monuments which lack "permanency," points of reference that promote stability without inhibiting primacy. American experience illustrates the triumph of reason and moderation, but by attributing unprecedented speed to New World history, Cooper discharges the burden of the past.

Neither exclusively a defense of tradition nor an assault on entailment, *The Pioneers* is a contradictory work which aspires toward the simultaneous enactment of both of those intentions. That is not to suggest that on its surface *The Pioneers'* narrative is fractured or that its conclusion is uncertain. On the contrary, H. Daniel Peck's description of Cooper's landscapes as intensely formal compositions is equally applicable to *The Pioneers'* narrative resolutions.[7]

7 H. Daniel Peck, *A World By Itself: The Pastoral Moment in Cooper's Fiction* (New Haven, 1977).

Cooper duly dispatches each of his characters and defuses
all of the novel's conflicts. As Edgar Dryden has argued
in a discussion of the Littlepage Trilogy, Cooper assumes
in his historical fiction the role of temporal detective.[8] Having investigated the puzzle of the past, he assigns motive,
imputes casuality, and imposes a rational system on the
flux of time. As historian and novelist, Cooper excavates
and buries, stresses and excludes, to construct a frame within which human experience has value and coherence.

And yet, the resolutions Cooper crafts to achieve that
certainty are not convincing. Judge Temple's disputes with
the novel's other characters reproduce the polar conflict between originality and derivation which complicates Cooper's historiographic objectives. As a figure of order and
transition, the Judge represents temporal inscription. If any
of the characters who resist Temple's authority successfully
displace him, continuity is broken and originality becomes
possible. One of Cooper's competing imperatives would
thereby be realized. But such a triumph would invalidate
Cooper's efforts to shape a controlling context. By severing
his generation and his culture from fixed principles of
temporal development, Cooper would define history as
entirely random and cast doubt on the security of America's
future. Conversely, should Temple's power prove sufficient to check his rivals, Cooper would place himself in the
position of rejecting the prospect of a national departure
from the past.

Rather than engaging this impasse, Cooper represses
its force by denying a clear victory to any of his characters.

---

8 Edgar Dryden, "History and Progress: Some Implications of Form in
Cooper's Littlepage Novels," *Nineteenth-Century Fiction* 26 (June 1971):
49–64.

In the novel's concluding chapters, the settlers of Templeton are compelled to acknowledge civil authority. The most restive among them are exiled to the frontier, while those who remain are transformed by their growing wealth and intelligence. But the settlers' ability to evade Temple's laws throughout the rest of the novel undermines Cooper's assurance of their conversion. The specter of frontier anarchy continues to haunt *The Pioneers* despite Cooper's efforts to contain the villagers' freedom. Paradoxically, the disruptive energies of Templeton's citizens, which Cooper struggles to defuse, become the agency through which he restrains the intimidating power of historical precedent.

Cooper's response to Natty and Chingachgook's quarrel with Judge Temple is marked by a similar ambivalence. Although he consistently describes them as anachronisms whose departure from the field of the novel is both inevitable and desirable, Natty and Chingachgook remain more attractive figures than Temple or the settlers who supplant them. Their respect for the wilderness and their commitment to principle stand in stark contrast to the greed of the villagers and to the expediency of the Judge. Their grievances are discharged, but that resolution does not alleviate the sense of loss Cooper associates with their exile. Without diminishing his rational support for the progress Temple introduces, Cooper retains an emotional commitment to Natty and Chingachgook as figures who limit Temple's stature and appeal.

Oliver Effingham's rivalry with Judge Temple is dismissed as the product of misunderstanding. The rebellious son succeeds, through the contrivances of Cooper's narrative, a limiting father, while paternal authority is simultaneously preserved. Judge Temple is not literally banished; he continues to control his property. He does, however, disappear from the novel. In *The Pioneers'* final chapter Effingham replaces him as the novel's dominant figure without having committed the parricide which seems inevitable throughout the rest of Cooper's narrative. Rather than enacting that threatened assault, Cooper merely removes Temple from the novel's stage to its wings and installs Effingham in the Judge's place. History proceeds without disruption; a new world is called into being through a "magical change."

Despite the skill with which Cooper reconciles *The Pioneers'* tensions, the reader's difficulties remain. The impossibility of being free from, and bound to, history is only temporarily obscured. By denigrating Temple's achievements and distancing his world from that of the present Cooper establishes his generation's originality. He compromises, however, the true basis of that freedom from the past by replacing the peculiarly American world of Judge Temple with a social milieu which lacks a national specificity. The thriving villages of contemporary New York would not be out of place in England, or for that matter, in rural France or Switzerland. With the departure of Natty Bumppo, Chingachgook, Judge Temple, and the unruly settlers of Templeton, cultural originality evaporates. Cooper's temporal acceleration forces frontier America into the dimly remembered past and reproduces in the brief expanse of national time the refinement of centuries of European experience.

In *The Pioneers'* concluding scene, Natty pays a final visit to the graves of Chingachgook and Major Effingham —the representatives of the cultural collision that has generated American history—and then leaves Templeton for the wilderness. Judge Temple is absent, reduced to insignificance by Oliver Effingham's enfranchisement. His daughter and Effingham bid farewell to Natty and assume possession of his estate. This conclusion significantly tempers the novel's claims for national particularity. Cooper has established his culture's independence by locating America's beginnings in the unprecedented confrontations of the frontier, but he has discharged the provinciality and the turmoil inherent in that origin by displacing it to a remote past. The America of the novel's present is the product of the nation's pioneering history, but it has progressed beyond its roots to duplicate European achievement. Oliver Effingham and not Natty Bumppo or Judge Temple becomes the novel's representative American. Cooper attempts to preserve national autonomy by insisting that Effingham is a synthetic figure who embodies the values of Temple, Bumppo, and Chingachgook, as well as the sophistication of his English heritage. But the Effingham who dominates the novel's final scenes bears little or no resemblance to his American fathers. He is a gentleman whose tastes are more suited to the courts of London and Paris than to the cabins of the frontier.

Cooper's erasure of American difference is most apparent in his use of aristocratic imagery. The mock-heroic quality he attributes to early Templeton is clearly ironic. Marmaduke Temple's nickname is "Duke," Templeton's leading citizens are "nobles," and at one point in the novel, Richard Jones refers to the Judge as a "King." The discrepancy between that imagery and the humble reality of Templeton is unmistakable. By employing a chivalric motif to describe the American frontier, Cooper emphasizes difference and historical rupture. But when he repeatedly refers to Temple's daughter Elizabeth as "the heiress," his intentions are far from satiric. Elizabeth and Effingham, whom Cooper describes as an appropriate consort for an American princess, are nobles in actuality. The world they govern differs from that of Europe only in the matters of title and hereditary privilege. But by installing a British heir as the ruler of Templeton, Cooper erodes even that assumption of American distinction. The Judge's patent is Effingham's by right of birth. Unlike Temple, he has not acquired his wealth and position through effort and ingenuity but through inheritance and marriage. The open society of Temple's youth has solidified. Power is no longer the prize of conquest but the legacy of birth.

Cooper generalizes Effingham's recovery of his grandfather's lands by arguing that in colonial America the second generation of powerful families lost their positions to "the more active energies of a class whose exertions had been stimulated by necessity." But the third generation of these families, he continues, were inspired by "a healthful and active desire to emulate the character, the condition, and, peradventure, the wealth of their ancestors," and began "to re-ascend in the scale of society" (31). The fluidity of colonial America, a fundamental determinant of national difference, has then, Cooper maintains, given way to a more rigid social fabric within which families of noble descent have reclaimed their traditional privilege. It is certainly true that *The Pioneers* records the passing of monarchy—the reverses of George III and Louis XVI are noted in its text—but Effingham's ascendancy diminishes the extent of that social revolution. Aristocratic rule has been broken in America, but an analogous system has replaced it.

The all-embracing order of *The Pioneers'* conclusion

is also compromised by Cooper's reliance on negation as a narrative strategy. Like many other American writers from William Bradford to Norman Mailer, Cooper created space for his own writing by stressing the absence of a national context. Anticipating Hawthorne and James, in particular, Cooper argued that in America "there are no annals for the historian; no follies (beyond the most vulgar and commonplace) for the satirist; no manners for the dramatist; no obscure fictions for the writer of romance; no gross and hardy offences against decorum for the moralist; nor any of the rich artificial auxiliaries of poetry. . . . There is no costume for the peasant (there is scarcely a peasant at all), no wig for the judge, no baton for the general, no diadem for the chief magistrate." Even "the weakest hand," he argued, "can extract a spark from the flint, but it would baffle the strength of a giant to attempt kindling a flame with a pudding-stone."[9]

Cooper's negation of a context which might restrict his imaginative freedom had a liberating effect, but his willingness to avoid complexity and contradiction in the interests of coherence compromises the integrity of his writing. Cooper's characteristic response to the troubling characters and conflicts of *The Pioneers* is dismissal. Chingachgook dies, Natty sets off for the wilderness, disruptive settlers relocate westward, and Temple disappears from the novel's stage. Cooper explains their departure as a product of mutability, but narrative closure and not progress is the true source of their eclipse. Rather than granting the constancy of social tension, Cooper invokes the transformations of time to support his hermetic conclusion. Effingham

9 James Fenimore Cooper, *Notions of the Americans Picked Up by a Travelling Bachelor* (New York, 1963), 2:108–9.

never demonstrates his ability to quell the turmoil that troubled Judge Temple's reign. His acquisition of Temple's land is followed immediately by the conventional assurances of a happy ending. If *The Pioneers* were a novel of manners, Cooper's failure to document Effingham's successful administration of Templeton would present no serious difficulty. Surely it is possible to imagine the suspension of conflict in a specific frontier community. But Cooper predicates both America's future security and his historiographic perspective on Effingham's achievements. By refusing to engage the precarious quality of Oliver's authority, Cooper confuses the particular with the general. Brandishing the magic wand of history, he represses problems which do not admit a certain solution.

By emphasizing the doubled nature of *The Pioneers'* historical perspective, I am, to a limited degree, reaffirming a long-standing assessment of the novel. Most of Cooper's critics have centered their discussions of *The Pioneers* on the ambivalent character of the novel's conflicts. The Judge's quarrel with Natty Bumppo has, for example, been perceived as an expression of Cooper's wavering response to national progress. Torn between a commitment to social refinement and an attraction to the primitive, Cooper— readers such as D. H. Lawrence and Marvin Meyers have argued—first re-creates that tension in Judge Temple's confrontation with Natty Bumppo, and then through Oliver Effingham's mediation of their rivalry, suggests that American development need not imply the destruction of the values he associates with the wilderness.[10]

10 D. H. Lawrence, *Studies in Classic American Literature* (New York, 1961), 47–63; Marvin Meyers, *The Jacksonian Persuasion: Politics and Belief* (Stanford, 1960), 57–100.

Although this interpretation of *The Pioneers* provides a useful access to the novel's concerns, its scope is unnecessarily narrow. By describing *The Pioneers* as a didactic work in which Cooper advances an idealized version of what frontier settlement might and should become, this analysis neglects the novel's historiographic dimension. Cooper is not interested principally either in providing a model of sound social practice or in indulging a fantasy but is, instead, attempting to plot a system of causality. In the course of that effort, he employs Effingham's reconciliation of the Judge's dispute with Natty as an example of the dialectical process that has given American history its shape. It is as an illustration of that determining matrix and not as the locus of Cooper's primary thematic concern that the Judge's relationship with Natty acquires significance. Furthermore, such a reading of *The Pioneers* conflates Cooper's generational structure. Temple and Natty are not finally competitors but are parallel figures. By balancing the conflicting demands of progress and tradition, the Judge does not repudiate but, rather, refines the synthesis Natty has forged between Indian and European culture.

In his incisive study of the psychological sources of Cooper's artistry, Stephen Railton offers another explanation for *The Pioneers'* duality.[11] Extending Henry Nash Smith's observation that the novel's energies are primarily oedipal, Railton argues that Oliver Effingham's dealings with Judge Temple reenact Cooper's own family romance.[12] Cooper's ambivalent treatment of the Judge, Railton maintains, is an expression of his conflicting desires to submit to

11 Stephen Railton, *Fenimore Cooper: A Study of His Life and Imagination* (Princeton, 1978), 75–113.
12 Smith, 67. Also see Peck, 102–7.

his late father's authority and to overturn William Cooper's primacy. That argument seems to me to be unassailable. Indeed, it is hardly necessary to resort to Freudian terminology to support its assumptions. Cooper's abject failure to duplicate or even to preserve his father's achievements as a land developer, a political leader, and a capable provider present sufficient grounds for reading *The Pioneers* as an exercise in paternal displacement.[13] At the same time, Cooper's devotion to his father's memory and his deeply felt need to establish the significance of his lineage urged him toward a celebration of William Cooper's accomplishments.[14] Cooper's difficult relationship with his father-in-law, John Peter De Lancey, which Railton details, lends additional weight to his reading of the novel's tensions. De Lancey, whose social position was considerably more secure than Cooper's own, had deeded a portion of his Westchester estate to Cooper and his daughter Susan. Through a series of mismanaged transactions, Cooper lost that land and was forced to rely on De Lancey to discharge his debts.[15] As he wrote *The Pioneers*, Cooper was confronted not only by his failure to preserve William Cooper's estate and by his own financial reverses but also by the contempt of his father-in-law. It is reasonable to assume, therefore, that

13 For an account of Cooper's early failures, see *The Letters and Journals of James Fenimore Cooper*, ed. James Franklin Beard (Cambridge, Mass., 1960–68), 1:23–108. Hereafter this edition of Cooper's correspondence will be cited as *L&J*.

14 See George Dekker's discussion of Cooper's heritage in *James Fenimore Cooper the Novelist* (London, 1967), 6–19.

15 In an unpublished essay delivered at the State University College of New York at Oneonta, James H. Pickering detailed the complicated transactions through which Cooper mortgaged on three separate occasions the Hickories, a farm which had been owned by the Heathcote-De Lancey family since the early eighteenth century. For a discussion of Cooper's final rupture with his wife's family, see *L&J* 1:87n.

his fictional creation of a powerful father figure was complicated by his status as an unsuccessful son.

But regardless of the accuracy of Railton's description
of Cooper's psychic terrain, his argument has the effect of
diminishing the novel's resonance. Just as a reading of *The
Pioneers* which stresses Cooper's ambivalent conception
of progress addresses one rather limited aspect of his vision
of American history, Railton's analysis subordinates a more
comprehensive sense of generational entailment to the particular circumstances of Cooper's relation to his father. The
burden imposed by European cultural imperialism is, for
example, as pressing a concern in *The Pioneers* as is the
specter of William Cooper's authority. Like most of his
contemporaries, Cooper bitterly resented the subordinate
status of American culture. Across his career, he defended
national autonomy and attacked both European arrogance
and American subservience. The objective of his writing,
he argued, was to declare "the mental independence of
his nation"[16] and "to illustrate and enforce the peculiar
principles of his own country."[17] Even in his later polem-
ical works, such as *A Letter to His Countrymen* (1834)
and *The American Democrat* (1838) which record his
disillusionment with American society, Cooper refutes
European standards of judgment and reserves his harshest
criticism for Americans besotted by aristocratic pretension
and foreign opinion. His career, he argued in the *Letter*,
had been directed toward overturning a cultural dependence
"which should it continue to prevail must render every
American more or less subject to the views of those who are

16 Ibid., 2:84.
17 James Fenimore Cooper, *A Letter to His Countrymen* (New York,
1834), 98.

hostile to the prospects, the character and the power of his native land." For his own part, he regretted that in *Precaution* he had "fallen into the track of imitation," an error which, he argued, he had "endeavored to repair. . . . by providing a work [*The Spy*] that should be purely American and of which love of country should be the theme."[18]

Cooper's rejection of European cultural and literary models was intensified by his rivalry with Walter Scott. Beginning with the publication of *The Spy*, reviewers had termed him "the American Scott," a title which Cooper maintained "gives me more disgust than any other."[19] Time and again Cooper struggled to distance his writing from the Waverley Novels. He distinguished, for example, his work from Scott's as the divergent productions of a republican and an aristocrat,[20] cited Scott's unwillingness to engage American material,[21] and characterized his rather harshly reviewed novel, *The Heidenmauer* (1832), as better than two-thirds of the Waverley Novels.[22]

In a review of Lockhart's posthumous edition of Scott's *Memoir* (1837), Cooper codified his rejection of Scott's literary paternity. Seizing the occasion to assess Scott's character rather than the merits of the volume itself, Cooper attempted to "settle down" and "lessen the blind respect" an international public had accorded Scott by exposing in his life "motives that are never admitted by the upright, and never avowed by the sensitive." To that end, Cooper accused Scott of reviewing his own work, basing critical

18 Cooper, *A Letter to His Countrymen*, 4.
19 *L&J* 2:84.
20 Ibid., 310.
21 Ibid., 170.
22 Ibid., 310.

judgments on political expediency, deceiving the public
about the partisan character of the *Quarterly Review*,
slavishly defending aristocratic privilege, cheating his credi-
tors, courting personal favor through insincere praise, cal-
lously neglecting his wife and brother, and cruelly betray-
ing confidences in his diary. "It must require the credulity
of a believer in Animal Magnetism, or in Mormonism,"
Cooper concluded, "to think [Scott] a man of high moral
sensibilities, upright mind, simple practices or ingenious
habits."[23] Having maligned Scott's character, Cooper described his fiction as work which lacked originality, displayed
only a limited imaginative range, and dangerously glossed
aristocratic privilege. Cooper defended the extent of his
attack by arguing that Scott's reactionary views disqualified
him as a suitable writer for American and indeed for nineteenth-century audiences. His reputation must, he insisted,
be subjected to rigorous scrutiny and reappraisal.

But Cooper's efforts to counter the authority of Europe
in general and of Walter Scott in particular were, like his
assault on Judge Temple, balanced by a regard for context.
Despite his militant support for republican principles in
the abstract, he attacked American culture in the concrete as
an enshrinement of the mediocre. On one hand, Cooper
adamantly rejected European society as corrupt and, as
such, an unworthy model for America; and on the other, he
argued for standards of taste and conduct which would
permit the nation to approximate more closely the refinement of the Old World. In *The American Democrat*,
Cooper tried to resolve this contradictory response to European example in much the same way that he engaged the

23 *Knickerbocker* 12 (October 1838): 349–56.

historiographic inconsistencies of *The Pioneers.*[24] Blurring
the duality of his conception of America's proper relation
to Europe, he advanced a notion of the American gentleman as the arbiter of cultural direction. That paragon would
defend national autonomy, while he promoted the improvement of American manners. Every aspect of his life—his
home, his gardens, his dress, and his deportment—would
exemplify aristocratic taste. But because his political principles were those of a republican, Cooper's gentleman would
foster a form of social growth which would distinguish
American life from that of Europe. Like Oliver Effingham,
the American gentleman Cooper imagined would be inside
and outside history, an extension of, and a departure from,
all that had gone before.

Cooper's response to the burden of Walter Scott's example parallels his complex conception of America's relation to Europe. Despite his avowed contempt for Scott,
Cooper scrupulously defended their kinship. In his correspondence and his journals he duly recorded Scott's praise
for his writing, noting in a letter to his wife, for example,
that Scott "declared a person you love had more genius
than any living writer."[25] Far from rejecting Scott as
a dangerous reactionary, Cooper cultivated their friendship
and labored to secure an American copyright for Scott's
work.[26] Six months before he published his review of the
Memoir in the *Knickerbocker*, Cooper wrote a lengthy and
extensively documented letter to the editors of that journal explaining Scott's insulting description of his manners

---

24 James Fenimore Cooper, *The American Democrat* (Baltimore, 1969).
See, in particular, Cooper's remarks on the disadvantages of democratic
government and on the duties of station, 118–54.

25 *L&J* 3:327.

26 Ibid. 1:170–81, 224–27; 3:318–20.

in the *Memoir* as the result of Scott's confusion. The extent of the two writers' friendship must not, he insisted, be mistaken because of an unfortunate entry in Scott's diary.[27]

Cooper's concurrent efforts to defend and to disavow his association with Scott are as present in his fiction as they are in his correspondence and reviews. The ambivalence of Cooper's historical perspective in *The Pioneers* is itself an indication of his tangled relation with Scott. Regardless of Scott's debts to the antiquarian tradition and to the speculative sociology of Adam Ferguson, the Waverley Novels are primarily the product of the Edinburgh Enlightenment and of its commonsense philosophy.[28] Like Ferguson, Dugald Stewart, and William Robertson, whose thought he absorbed, Scott repudiated the skepticism of Hume and adopted a vision of history that was synthetic in its assumptions and didactic in its aims. He conceptualizes history as a series of conflicts between reason and fanaticism, defines the present as the product of the former's triumph, and regards historiography as a public service directed toward the preservation of order and moderate progress. The lessons of the Waverley Novels are clear. Reason is the basis of cultural development; the middle course is the avenue of growth. Tradition must be respected, but not at the expense of progress. By advancing his polemic in novels which are also histories, Scott not only teaches by example but also elevates an ideological position to the status of historical fact. Continuity, the Waverley Novels argue, is a cultural absolute. The disruption of the histori-

27 Ibid. 3:317–23.
28 For a thorough discussion of the historiographic assumptions which inform Scott's writing see Avrom Fleishman, *The English Historical Novel* (Baltimore, 1971), 37–101, and Duncan Forbes, "The Rationalism of Sir Walter Scott," *Cambridge Journal* 7 (1953–54): 19–31.

cal process by either reactionary or revolutionary elements is not only destructive but is ultimately futile.

By adopting in *The Pioneers*, the narrative formula and the ideological assumptions of the Waverley Novels, Cooper implicitly links his writing with Scott's. Like the novel's epigraphs which locate *The Pioneers* within the British literary tradition, Cooper's reliance on the form and vision of Scott's fiction establishes an international context for his writing. No mere provincial, Cooper becomes a co-equal of Scott, a fellow heir of a common literary tradition. But Cooper does not permit the historical perspective he derives from Scott to stand unchallenged. By imaginatively distancing the world of Judge Temple, he disrupts historical paternity while he preserves the security of that context. In qualifying *The Pioneers'* argument in this fashion, Cooper redefines his status vis-à-vis the Waverley Novels. *The Pioneers* builds on Scott's work but also departs from it by defending the originality of Oliver Effingham.

The literary anxiety of influence which *The Pioneers* records is, however, as subordinate an issue in the novel as Cooper's oedipal revolt against his father. Both of these concerns are fully subsumed by the cultural dynamic I have described. The particular tensions Cooper experienced as the son of William Cooper and the rival of Walter Scott only intensified the broadly defined generational pressures of his age. Oliver Effingham's status as both father and son does represent a fictive solution to a personal dilemma, but more significantly, it focuses the irresolvable longings of Cooper's contemporaries to be free from, and bound to, the past. Although my primary intention is to locate *The Pioneers* within that generational crisis, it is well worth noting that Cooper's efforts to blur the contradictions implicit in his historical perspective are not unique to the 1820s but reproduce a duality present throughout American letters. Whether one engages that doubled vision in John Winthrop's struggle to define the Puritan community as a New Jerusalem, a repudiation of European corruption and an event grounded by a providential context; in the ambivalence of Emerson's sense of the past, which this chapter's epigraphs record; or in the contradictory celebration and denial of history which marked the public rhetoric of the bicentennial, the syntax of national historiography remains remarkably consistent. Regardless of their place in time or their particular social and psychological contexts, American writers have continually affirmed and denied their connections to the past.

In arguing for the paradigmatic status of *The Pioneers* however, I do not wish to overstate the novel's significance. *The Pioneers* does illustrate a recurrent pattern of national vision, but it fails to explore the diametrically opposed desires inherent in that structure of feeling. An example rather than an analysis of America's doubled conception of the burden of history, the novel lacks self-consciousness and remains a fragmented work. As Cooper recrafts *The Pioneers'* narrative in the subsequent volumes of the Leatherstocking Tales, he becomes increasingly more aware of the contradictions that impede his efforts to plot America's past and ceases to repress them. By the conclusion of the Leatherstocking series, Cooper's fiction offers both a coherent exposition of national history and an insightful meditation on the duality of American consciousness.

~~2~~

"A Man without a Cross": *Mohicans* and the Cyclic Course of Empire

~~~~~

The first colonists saw in America an opportunity to regenerate their fortunes, their spirits, and the power of their church and nation; but the means to that regeneration ultimately became the means of violence, and the myth of regeneration through violence became the structuring metaphor of the American experience.

—*Richard Slotkin*, Regeneration through Violence

Since then, continued the Genius, with renewed energy, since the experience of past ages is lost for the living—since the errors of progenitors have not instructed their descendants, the ancient examples are about to reappear; the earth will see renewed the tremendous scenes it has forgotten. New revolutions will agitate nations and empires; powerful thrones will again be overturned, and terrible catastrophes will again teach mankind that the laws of nature and the precepts of wisdom and truth cannot be infringed with impunity.

—*Volney*, The Ruins

IN *Pages and Pictures from the Writings of James Fenimore Cooper* (1861), her survey of her father's literary career, Susan Cooper tells us that *The Last of the Mohicans* (1826) was the result of a pledge Cooper made to Edward Stanley during an 1825 tour of the Lake George region of New York. Cooper, Stanley, and five other British gentle-

45

men were impressed by the natural splendor of Glenn's Falls, and when Stanley observed that "here was the very scene for a romance," Cooper promised to compose such a work at his earliest convenience. Immediately after the conclusion of the tour, Cooper set himself to work on *Mohicans* and completed a draft of the novel four months after his return. He chose to set the tale in 1757 rather than in contemporary New York, Susan recalls, first, because he wanted to eliminate the dams which marred the beauty of the falls, and second, because he was interested in writing a romance which would be "essentially Indian in character."[1] His determination to reintroduce Natty Bumppo and Chingachgook as principal characters in *Mohicans* was apparently a more difficult decision. He realized, Susan explains, that a work which featured characters "already familiar to the reader" was "a dangerous experiment," but after seeking his wife's advice, "the step was taken and Natty and Chingachgook were once more brought before the reader."[2]

Susan Cooper's account of the genesis of *Mohicans* notwithstanding, there was another, more compelling reason for Cooper to write the second volume of what would become the Leatherstocking Tales. The bankruptcy of his father's estate, the failure of his own investments, the additional responsibilities he had assumed after the premature deaths of his older brothers, and the needs of his growing family had placed a severe strain on Cooper's finances—a pressure he hoped to alleviate through the sales of his fiction. The commercial success of *The Spy*, *The Pioneers*,

1 Susan F. Cooper, *Pages and Pictures from the Writing of James Fenimore Cooper* (New York, 1861), 126.
2 Ibid., 128.

and *The Pilot* (1824)—a sea novel which centered on the
adventures of John Paul Jones during the revolutionary
war—firmly grounded that expectation. But when *Lionel
Lincoln* (1825), his fifth novel, failed to attract a significant readership, Cooper's optimism abated. Rather than
pursuing the thirteen-novel history of the Revolution,
which *Lionel Lincoln* was to have inaugurated, Cooper
decided to abandon the project.[3] Although *The Pioneers*
had sold fewer copies than either *The Spy* or *The Pilot*,
Natty and Chingachgook remained his most popular characters. By reimagining them as warriors at the height of
their manhood, Cooper might reasonably have hoped to
recapture public favor.

Cooper's rationale for reintroducing Natty and Chingachgook in *Mohicans* is, however, less significant than the
effect of that decision. Their presence in both *The Pioneers*
and in *Mohicans* establishes a particularly intimate relationship between the two novels, one which both enriches and
circumscribes our reading.[4] Natty's and Chingachgook's
destinies are present to us from the moment of their initial
appearance in *Mohicans*. Their values and their cultural
roles have been clearly defined. We know that they will
survive their adventures, that the battlefields they cross
will become the sights of "beautiful and thriving villages,"
and that their brotherhood will anticipate the cultural synthesis Oliver Effingham ultimately achieves. To some

---

3 Ibid., 101-2.
4 To a considerable degree, a writer's *oeuvre* is his text; each of his
novels a chapter in that larger work. But unlike the major novels of most
other writers, the Leatherstocking Tales articulate a narrative grammar in
which vocabulary—conceived of as character and incident—remains constant,
while syntax—Cooper's narrative strategies—vary. Both change and continuity within the series can be charted, therefore, in a highly focused
manner.

degree our prescience is a product of *Mohicans*' status as a historical novel. The decline of the Indian nations and the disruption of European hegemony are matters of public record. But our prior knowledge of the narrative progress of *Mohicans* is more precise than that. We understand that the tribes and the European armies of the novel will be displaced by American settlers, but we also know that whatever closure Cooper may effect in *Mohicans*, its resolutions are prefatory to the model of cultural development he advances in *The Pioneers*.[5]

The implications of this narrative continuity are quite crucial. Because we know that *Mohicans* is not an entirely self-contained work, because we recognize that the past which Cooper details in this novel will shape the subsequent events of *The Pioneers*, we are drawn toward an organic conception of American time and away from a reading of *Mohicans* as an exploration of a discrete historical period. Just as Oliver Effingham's links to the Old World of his grandfather and the New World of Judge Temple define a temporal continuum in *The Pioneers*, Natty and Chingachgook's reappearance in *Mohicans* establishes Cooper's perspective as progessive rather than episodic. Even more directly than Effingham, Natty and Chingachgook are transitional figures who explicitly bond the colonial America of 1757 with the independent nation of 1793.

Mohicans serves, however, not only as a preface to *The Pioneers* but also as an appendix. Cooper does employ Natty and Chingachgook to illustrate the unity of national time and to affirm America's organic relationship with

---

5 That is not to argue that the dialectical closure which Cooper effects in *Mohicans* is incomplete but that his resolution of cultural tension in this novel reinforces the historiographic paradigm he advances in *The Pioneers*.

Europe. Their kinship in general, and Natty's synthesis of a Christian and a savage perspective in particular, define an intermediate state of cultural development which has its roots in European exploration and settlement and its telos in the America of Oliver Effingham. But both their brotherhood and Natty's unique vision are without historical precedent and, as such, suggest a source for the nation's distinctive identity. Emblems of both continuity and departure, Natty and Chingachgook renew and extend the conceptual ambivalence of *The Pioneers*. Again we are confronted by a novel which describes America as a nation at once derivative and innovative. Cooper neither resolves nor fully acknowledges that paradox, but he does advance in *Mohicans* a newly imagined fictional strategy which reformulates the contradictory logic of *The Pioneers*.

By restoring Natty and Chingachgook to the prime of their lives, Cooper presses his investigation of America's origins beyond an autobiographical context to a more distant, prerevolutionary era of the national past. Rather than beginning *Mohicans* by describing the wilderness as a place of renewal and progress, as he does in *The Pioneers*, Cooper associates the America of 1757 with chaos and destruction. "There was," he writes, "no recess of the woods so dark nor any secret place so lovely, that it might claim exemption from the inroads of those who had pledged their blood to satiate the vengeance, or to uphold the cold and selfish policy of the distant monarchs of Europe."[6] Peace, was "unknown to this fatal region . . . its glades and glens rang with the sounds of martial music" (12). America,

6 James Fenimore Cooper, *The Last of the Mohicans* (Albany, N.Y., 1983), 11. Future references will be to this edition and will be cited by page number in the text.

Cooper observes, was never innocent of history. The Europeans who settled the continent did not leave their pasts behind them but transported their rivalries to the frontier. Although the final stage of the French and Indian Wars (1756–63), which *Mohicans* recounts, began in America and spread to Europe, the seventy-five-year course of that conflict (1698–1763) was, as Cooper reminds us, only a provincial episode of five centuries of French and British conflict.

And yet, Cooper's point is not simply that the French and Indian Wars were—like the colonial period they spanned—an extension of the European past, but that they were the fullest expression of the barbarity which marked that history. Far from tempering Old World conflicts, the American setting exacerbated them. The military codes which had somewhat restrained the ferocity of European warfare rapidly deteriorated in the wilderness. Massacres and scalpings replaced pitched battles and the exchange of colors; traditional conceptions of honor yielded to the exigencies of the forests. More important, in the wilderness, British and French combat was no longer a source of national unity but a divisive conflict in which loyalties were compromised and cultural values repeatedly transgressed.

The European armies of *Mohicans* are lost on the American frontier. Their lines of battle are uncertain, and their alliances with the native tribes are precarious. The boundaries of Old World principle are similarly obscured. The French commandant, General Montcalm, ostentatiously displays his chivalry by permitting an overmatched British force to surrender Fort William Henry without sacrificing their honor. But as the British troops withdraw, Montcalm's Indian allies attack and slaughter them. Enmeshed in a conflict in which the codes of European warfare do not apply, Montcalm passively observes the violation of his word and the destruction of his reputation. The American setting has an equally disruptive effect on the judgment of the British commander, General Webb. Shocked by prior ambushes and severed from the fixed rules of open combat, Webb refuses to relinquish the security of his stockade to relieve his besieged detachment at William Henry. Colonel Munro, William Henry's ranking officer, describes Webb's timidity as a betrayal that has brought dishonor to Britain and to his command. Broken by his surrender to Montcalm, Munro sadly observes that he never expected to live long enough to see "an Englishman afraid to support a friend" (165).

The warfare which *Mohicans* recounts is as corrosive for Indian values as it is for those of Europe. In much the same way that British and French conventions fall prey to expediency, Indian honor is a casualty of interracial combat. The Mohican and Iroquois warriors of the novel do not contend for territorial rights but for the favor of their European paymasters. Fueled by whiskey and honorary medallions, they violate their treaties and offer their services to the highest bidder. The taking of scalps becomes a commercial rather than a ceremonial practice; hereditary leaders are displaced by renegades who pander to the greed of their followers. Tribal involvement in a European feud is, of course, self-destructive. As allies of the British and the French, the Indians become the agents of their own annihilation. "White cunning," as Natty observes, has thrown "the tribes into great confusion, as respects friends and enemies; so that the Hurons and the Oneidas, who speak the same tongue . . . take each other's scalps" (196).

American settlement is not, then, a beacon of hope for human progress but the culmination of centuries of discord. Within the nation's forests, violence is unchecked by either principle or convention. Regression and not renewal is the product of Europe's encounter with the primitive. Cooper buttresses this assessment of America's origins in *Mohicans'* initial episode, a scene which epitomizes the dislocation implicit in the European adventure in the wilderness. In setting off from Fort Edward to escort Alice and Cora Munro to their father's encampment at William Henry, Duncan Heyward, an officer of the Royal Americans, recapitulates the thrust of European settlement in the New World. Persuaded by Magua, his Indian guide, that the Munro sisters will be safer apart from the main body of his troops, Heyward abandons the demarcations of the British road for the uncharted paths of the forest. His decision to trust Magua is manifestly foolish. He knows that the scout is a renegade from a tribe allied with the French and that he has been publicly lashed at Munro's order for his drunkenness, but he refuses to suspect Magua's motives because he is a fellow servant of the British empire.

The extravagance of Heyward's naïveté most certainly impairs *Mohicans'* plausibility. His willingness to place Alice and Cora's safety in Magua's hands seems more a fictional contrivance than a flaw of judgment.[7] It is, however, the extent of Heyward's blindness which Cooper wishes to emphasize. Heyward is incapable of recognizing

7 Cooper's implausible contrivances in *Mohicans*, and indeed in all of his novels, have been sharply criticized by many of his readers. He wrote, as Joseph Conrad remarked, "before the birth of the great American language," and like his diction, his narratives are bound by European conventions disjunctive with his subjects and settings. Cooper's occasional clumsiness does not, however, impair the clarity of his vision but illuminates the difficulties he encountered as he struggled to frame a national discourse.

Magua's obvious malice, not because he is a fool, but because convention rather than logic governs his conduct. Cooper counters the potential skepticism of his readers and generalizes Heyward's error by recalling General Braddock's defeat at Fort Duquesne in an earlier battle of the war. Braddock, Cooper notes, rejected the advice of George Washington, his colonial aide, and marched on the French encampment at the Ohio as if he were on a parade ground. A small band of Indians and French regulars fired with impunity into the British ranks, killing Braddock and routing his troops.[8] Although Heyward profits from Braddock's example by adopting the circumvention Magua suggests, like Braddock, he imposes a European grid on the forests. Because Magua is a British scout, Heyward assumes that he is worthy of his trust. All other considerations are subordinated to the power of that flawed conception. As a colonial officer, Heyward's weakness is more troubling than Braddock's recalcitrance. He has not, despite his American birth, acquired a vision adequate to his circumstance but has passively adopted an Old World perspective. The price of that mistake is death.

In beginning *Mohicans* with this episode, Cooper announces two fundamental assumptions. First, Heyward's rash decision establishes the controlling force of history. As vulnerable in the forests as General Braddock, Heyward is indeed a Royal American, a living example of the New World's failure to effect difference and separation. Second, Cooper uses Heyward's journey into the wilderness to argue that historical inscription is as damaging as it is limiting. Heyward's reliance on European convention not only

8 See Harold Rosenberg's insightful analysis of the resonance of Braddock's defeat in *The Tradition of the New* (New York, 1959), 13–22.

impairs his judgment but also leaves him incapable of either defending Alice and Cora or preserving his own life. Bound by the past, Heyward has no future. The only prospect for his survival and for that of the nascent culture he represents is a denial of history, a renunciation of the European assumptions that have polluted the forests with blood. That independence, Cooper argues, cannot be realized by adopting native customs. The British and the French armies of *Mohicans* only accelerate their destruction by forging alliances with the Indians. Montcalm and Webb are faced with the loss of their reputations not only because they fail to adapt to American circumstances but also because they link their destinies to the savage practices of the tribes. By enlisting the Indians in their conflict, they become, regardless of their imagined detachment, the sponsors of bloodshed and destruction.

Cooper stresses the pernicious effects of this cultural slippage by detailing at some length the personal history of Colonel Munro. A victim of rigid European social conventions, Munro has been denied the hand of the woman he loved. Impelled by that rejection to leave his native Scotland, he joins a British regiment in the West Indies where he marries a woman of mixed blood. Such a marriage, Cooper observes, would have been unthinkable in Britain, but severed from that restraining context, Munro adopts the less certain values of the islands. His liaison has tragic consequences both for his reputation and for his daughter Cora. Racially impure, she is a social outcast and the source of Munro's enduring guilt. Just as he generalizes Heyward's mistaken judgment by introducing the example of General Braddock, Cooper locates Munro's weakness against a cultural referent. The Colonel's West Indian

marriage has resulted, he maintains, not simply from
Munro's moral laxity but from England's involvement
in the slave trade. Both the Colonel's presence in the islands
and the social climate which sanctions miscegenation are
the products of national compromise. By abandoning principle to reap the financial rewards of slavery, Britain has
sacrificed its integrity as surely as Munro has hazarded his
honor and his daughter's happiness.

Cooper presents, then, the European position in America as untenable. By rigidly preserving an Old World perspective, the British and the French fail to realize the New
World's potential for renewal and become the victims of
their obstinacy. But by abandoning civilized restraints
to fight with and like the Indians, they become savages unworthy of any victory they might achieve. In *Mohicans'*
second episode, however, Cooper frames a third possibility
for American development. As Magua leads Heyward,
Alice, and Cora deeper into the forest, the party encounters
the camp of Natty, Chingachgook, and Uncas, Chingachgook's son. Natty immediately detects Magua's treachery
and warns Heyward of his danger. Unswayed by Heyward's assurance that Magua "serves with our forces as a
friend" (37), Natty argues that "a Mingo is a Mingo" and
tells Heyward that a single glance has been sufficient to
convince him of Magua's intentions (39). Natty is capable
of such certain judgment because he has repudiated both
the conventional assumptions of Heyward and Braddock
and the moral relativism of Colonel Munro. He has not
been, as he later tells Heyward, "too proud to learn from
the wit of a native" and can, therefore, prosper in the wilderness (206). But in acquiring that knowledge, Natty has
not lapsed into savagery. As he continually insists, he is "a

man without a cross," a character whose values are determined by the natural law of the forests and not by the
historically bound codes of either the Europeans or the
Indians (70).

By describing Natty as a man apart, Cooper restructures
the priorities of *The Pioneers*. In that novel, Cooper's concern for social stability led him to emphasize Natty's role
as a figure of continuity, an intermediary between the
divergent traditions of his narrative. In *Mohicans*, Cooper
continues to promote an organic conception of time, but here
he places much greater stress on Natty's independence from
history. His separation from the contending cultures of the
novel—and not his synthetic function—is the crucial aspect
of his character. Regardless of this shift in emphasis, Natty's
primary function in Cooper's fiction remains constant. He
is, as he was in *The Pioneers*, a figurative as well as a literal
guide whose immunity from the temptations of both the
forests and the camps defines a model for national growth.
Only by adopting Natty's uncoded vision can Heyward
and young America survive the destruction which claims
Mohicans' European and Indian warriors.

But Natty's capacity to redirect the course of national
history is again restricted by his celibacy. Childless and unsuited to the settlements, he cannot directly promote cultural progress. If his life is to have meaning, his values must
be assimilated by a socially engaged character. Initially,
that transmission seems impossible within the narrative
frame of *Mohicans*. Unlike Oliver Effingham, whose kinship with Natty predates the opening of *The Pioneers*, Duncan Heyward is resistant to Natty's influence. Even after
he has been convinced of Magua's treachery, he refuses to
permit Natty to kill the renegade because "he may be in-

nocent" (40). Rejecting Natty's argument that "whoever comes into the woods to deal with the natives must use Indian fashions," he attempts unsuccessfully to overpower Magua and hold him captive until a court martial can be convened (40). Superficially, Heyward's scruples suggest his moral superiority. In fact, his reluctance to kill Magua is only another example of his unquestioning adherence to European conventions. Heyward's chivalry, like that of Montcalm, is a mask which disguises the savage enterprise in which he is involved. He may wish to treat Magua fairly, but his ultimate mission is the destruction of the tribes. Natty serves with the British forces, but unlike Heyward and his superior officers, he understands that "nothing but vast wisdom and onlimited power should dare to sweep off men in multitudes" (184). He is ready to "extarminate" hostile warriors (112) and can, without hesitation, drive his knife through an enemy's "naked bosom to the heart," but he predicates that violence on abstract notions of good and evil and not on political or economic imperatives (71). As rigorous as the wilderness circumstances that have formed it, Natty's virtue is militant, but it is virtue nonetheless.

Heyward's inability to act on the basis of a similarly unclouded perspective continues to compromise his security. Spared by Heyward's reliance on alien conventions, Magua rallies his war party and intercepts the company as they continue on their way to William Henry. Surrounded at Glenn's Falls by Magua's braves and out of ammunition, Natty and Heyward again quarrel over strategy. The women, Natty argues, must be temporarily abandoned while new ammunition is secured. Cora supports Natty's judgment and tells Heyward that "this is not a time for idle

subtleties and false opinions, but a moment when every
duty should be equally considered. To us you can be of no
further service here" (80). Heyward admits that he is
powerless, but he insists on remaining with the sisters while
Natty and the Mohicans escape. Natty's wisdom is, of
course, confirmed. Heyward, Alice, Cora, and David
Gamut, a choirmaster who has joined their party, are captured and prepared for torture. But Natty, Chingachgook,
and Uncas have rearmed and, at a climactic moment, burst
into Magua's camp and free his prisoners.

The melodramatic quality of this rescue is crucial to
Cooper's intentions. In describing Heyward's misguided
chivalry, Cooper is not exploiting an overworked romantic
cliché for its emotional appeal but is quite consciously de-
constructing that convention. Anticipating Mark Twain's
ironic attack on the Waverley Novels as a principal cause
of the Civil War, Cooper rejects Heyward's dependence
on a European model of conduct as destructive for America's interests. Heyward's gallantry, in short, does not type
him as Cooper's hero but as Natty's foil, a man entirely
given to "idle subtleties and false opinions." If the culture
Heyward represents is to survive, he must adopt a new
species of vision. By refusing to abandon European convention, he belies his birth and proves himself incapable of
discharging the primary functions of any society—the defense of women and the preservation of security.

By establishing, at this point in his narrative, Heyward's conversion as a necessary condition of American
progress, Cooper defines *Mohicans* as a novel of initiation
and, in doing so, seemingly limits both his narrative and his
historiographic options. Either Heyward will renounce his
adolescent dependence on European standards and initiate

a new cultural direction, or he will remain the victim of the past and invalidate the prospect of American originality. The precedent of *The Pioneers* suggests that Cooper will choose the first of these two alternatives. We assume that Heyward, like Oliver Effingham, will displace the novel's patriarchs and become the progenitor of a distinctive American history. On one level, *Mohicans'* conclusion fulfills that expectation. Having demonstrated his growth, Heyward claims Alice Munro as his bride and presides over the departure of the novel's father figures. America's future is placed in his hands; the nation's subsequent glory is assured.

The narrative strategy Cooper adopts to achieve this end differs considerably however, from that of *The Pioneers*. In that novel, Cooper's historiographic orientation is primarily melioristic. Although Oliver Effingham's acquisition of Judge Temple's estate demonstrates, for Cooper, the final realization of American autonomy, Effingham's ascendancy culminates a lengthy process of mediation and change. He is the heir of the nation's constituent traditions and embodies the synthetic character of American experience. Cooper, to be sure, qualifies Effingham's links to the past in an effort to reduce the burden of cultural and generational inscription which *The Pioneers'* progressive spirit admits. But that tension is repressed throughout the novel and is never fully present in its text. In *Mohicans*, Cooper's dual conception of American history as a departure from, and an extension of, the past becomes explicit. He does not respond to the narrative decision Heyward's rite of passage presents by choosing between the two options available to him, but offers instead parallel accounts which record, in turn, Heyward's failure to separate himself from the past and his achievement of an independent identity.

The first of these competing levels of discourse begins immediately after Natty has freed Duncan, Alice, and Cora from Magua's camp and climaxes in the William Henry massacre. Natty, who has demonstrated his authority by rescuing Heyward and the Munro sisters, charts the path they must follow in the forests. "Better and wiser would it be," he tells them, "if [men] could understand the signs of nature, and take a lesson from the fowls of the air, and the beasts of the field" (124). Books, and the inherited wisdom they record, he concludes, are unreliable guides which only obscure the truth he finds expressed "so clear in the wilderness" (117). Natty's advice is consistent with Cooper's call for the establishment of a distinctive American perspective, but his position is undermined during the rest of the journey to William Henry.

Because the landscape the party crosses has been broken by war, nature's "signs" no longer transmit eternal verities. The placid water of Lake George is not a text which may be read as a model of divine harmony but is an icon which recalls the brutal British victory over Baron Dieskau earlier in the war. The lake, which now bears the name "Bloody Pond," is haunted by history. The spirits of the dead and dying who were cast into its depths purportedly walk its shores and disrupt the forest's calms with their shrieks. Nor is the secluded mound on which Alice and Cora recline an instructive emblem of nature's tranquility. It is instead, Natty tells the sisters, a mass grave which he helped to dig some years before. The only lesson it can teach is the constancy of man's barbarism. Although "it seemed as if a vast range of country lay buried in eternal sleep," nightfall in the forests is not a harbinger of peace but a time of increased danger (134). "A mighty army," Natty cautions Heyward, is "at rest among yonder silent trees and barren mountains" (135). That presence redefines the significance of the "fleecy mantle" of fog that materializes as the dawn approaches. This curtain of rest becomes a shroud which masks the road to William Henry. There is, in short, Cooper concludes, no possibility of reading nature in the way Natty recommends. The signs of providential order which Natty once detected in the forest have been overlayed by history's impenetrable gloss. With the arrival of man, nature's transcendental code has receded to a point of absence. Not only is Duncan unable to "take a lesson" from the wilderness, but Natty, too, is now powerless to interpret its message. Confounded by what he terms man's "abuse of nature," he mistakes his direction and leads Heyward, Alice, and Cora away from William Henry and into the line of battle.

More by chance than by design, the party does reach the fort. Colonel Munro hears Alice's screams and orders his men to hold their fire in time to save their lives. But his rescue of his daughters is achieved at the expense of Natty's leadership. Heyward deserts him to rejoin his regiment; Alice and Cora flee from his protection to embrace their father. Natty's humiliation is complete. Departing almost immediately to seek reenforcements from Fort Edward, he is captured by the French and returned in disgrace to William Henry. Throughout the subsequent negotiations for Munro's surrender, he disappears from Cooper's narrative. Natty's dismissal from *Mohicans'* text bears a considerable thematic burden. His willful separation from the destructive conventions of European and Indian culture—a negation which Cooper has defined as the sole prospect for American renewal—has miscarried.

Like the novel's other characters, he is submerged by history. His efforts to guide Heyward's development have been futile. Nature itself has proven powerless to resist human presence.

Cooper explores the consequences of Natty's failure to transmit his vision to Duncan Heyward by detailing the events which precipitate the William Henry massacre. Surrounded by the French and faced with imminent destruction, Munro meets with Montcalm to discuss the terms of his surrender. The meeting of the two commanders proceeds with great formality: agreements are reached, and the honor of both sides is scrupulously preserved. Despite his courtesy, Montcalm's hypocrisy is apparent. He feigns an ignorance of English to gain a tactical advantage and lies about the strength of his forces. His willingness to permit Munro's troops to withdraw proceeds, Cooper suggests, more from hubris than humanity. But Montcalm's difference from Munro is largely superficial. Like Montcalm, Munro is obsessed with questions of reputation and protocol and is indifferent to the practical consequences of warfare. Both men are blind to the madness their armies promote, having disguised that horror with the empty forms of honor. Montcalm's Indian allies, among whom Magua is now a leader, have illusions of their own about the glories of battle, but they do not subscribe to the conventions of their European counterparts. When Munro accepts Montcalm's pledge of safe conduct and leads his troops from the fort, the Indians slaughter his column and recapture Alice and Cora.

Cooper does not mitigate the Indians' guilt. He describes them as "raging savages" who hover "at a distance like vultures" and, at Magua's command, descend on the fort's women and children with unrestrained ferocity.

"Heated and maddened" by the flow of English blood, they "kneeled to the earth, and drank freely, excitingly, hellishly, of the crimson tide" (176). But regardless of the extravagance of Cooper's rhetoric, his Indian characters are only the agents of the novel's carnage. Montcalm, who addresses them as his "children"; Munro, who also enlists the support of the tribes; and ultimately the governments the two leaders serve are the true authors of the William Henry massacre. The chivalric conventions of the French and British may disguise the horror of warfare more effectively than the codes of Indian combat, but the reality of their mission is the same. By scalping their victims and drinking their blood, the Indians unmask the violence at the core of human identity. Just as he defines Montcalm and Munro as parallel figures whose differences are inconsequential, Cooper links the white and red warriors at William Henry as characters driven by an identical will to power.

Cooper extends this assumption of the universality of human motivation to its logical conclusion by arguing that both the Indians and the Europeans of *Mohicans* are bound by the same historical process. Both cultures are, he maintains, organic entities subject to death. The youth of the tribes is spent; their dissolution is imminent.[9] Tamenund, the ancient Mohican chieftain, whose great age is emblematic of the status of tribal life, recognizes the inevitability of that eclipse and mourns the passing of his race. "In the morning," he tells his diminished people, "I saw the sons of Unâmis happy and strong; and yet, before the night has

9 Cooper's consideration of cultural decline is a constant feature of the novel. In one of *Mohicans*' initial episodes, Natty and Chingachgook discuss the disappearance of the tribes (33); in the tale's final sentence, Tamenund mourns the extinction of "the wise race of Mohicans" (350).

come, have I lived to see the last warrior of the wise race of the Mohicans" (350).[10] Cooper's European characters have not entered that final night of cultural experience, but their day too has passed. "The imbecility of her military leaders abroad, and the fatal want of energy in her councils at home," Cooper observes, "had lowered the character of Great Britain from the proud elevation on which it had been placed by the talents and enterprise of her former warriors and statesmen. No longer dreaded by her enemies, her servants were fast losing the confidence of self respect" (13). Britain's "mortifying abasement" and "degraded fortunes" are paralleled by the failure of the "restless enterprise of the French" (12). Impelled by his "attention to the forms of courtesy," Montcalm, Cooper writes, was induced two years after the events of the novel, "to throw away his life on the Plains of Abraham" (153). With that defeat, French hopes for a world empire were dealt a fatal blow. Their American conflict is, for the French and British, both a futile exercise—neither side "was destined to retain" the territories they contested—and a preamble to the eventual destruction of imperial power in the French and American revolutions (12).

This cyclic paradigm—a temporal design Cooper derives from protoromantic art, from Condorcet and Gibbon, and most immediately from Volney, whose *Les Ruines, ou méditations sur les révolutions des empires* (1791) enjoyed a great vogue in America—has far-reaching implications for the culture whose history Cooper charts. If men and the societies they create are governed by an organic

10 Chingachgook's son Uncas, the "last warrior" of whom Tamenund speaks, personifies Cooper's conception of the inescapable force of history. Despite his courage and his virtue, Uncas's death is inevitable from the beginning of Cooper's narrative.

process of growth and decline, America, as a nation of men, must be subject to the same temporal course. A new political entity may have emerged in the Revolution, but that beginning only initiates the same cyclic process which has led to the dissolution of the tribes and the debasement of Europe. Tamenund makes explicit that prospect when he warns that the white man should "not boast before the face of the Manito too loud. They entered the land at the rising, and may yet go off at the setting sun" (305). The one avenue of escape from that spiral of decline—the radical example of Natty Bumppo—has been lost. Heyward has remained loyal to the conventions of Europe and immune to Natty's influence. In the bloodshed of William Henry the determining power of history is affirmed. The potential for human renewal implicit in the wilderness is an illusion. Men are incapable of change; their history is an endlessly repeating decimal.

But Cooper immediately turns from this cyclic conception of human experience and doubles the thematic significance of William Henry. The massacre, which terminates the first half of *Mohicans* and forecloses the prospect of American originality, becomes, in the second half of the novel, a moment of cultural genesis. At William Henry, Cooper proceeds to argue, America's European and Indian ancestry was annihilated, clearing the way for the birth of a new national identity. Montcalm's reputation is forever tarnished, Munro's sanity is impaired by the guilt he experiences, the Indians are exposed as satanic figures who must be eliminated. Clearly, the traditions they represent have had no hand in the creation of "the beautiful and thriving villages" of *The Pioneers*. To account for that pastoral state, Cooper turns from the grim events of Wil-

liam Henry to describe the emergence of a new cultural
vision.

Cooper effects this reversal by rewriting the first half of
Mohicans.[11] In the aftermath of William Henry, Natty
reclaims the position of authority he occupied at the beginning of the novel and organizes a search party to rescue the
kidnapped Alice and Cora. As Natty, Chingachgook, and
Uncas lead Heyward and Munro into the forests, Cooper
reconstitutes Natty's pre–William Henry relationship with
Heyward. Natty is once more the peerless guide; Heyward
is again the resistant disciple who relies on British judgment
to guide his conduct. Duncan admits that Natty's skills as
a tracker are superior to his own but disputes his leadership
because, as a captain of the Royal Americans, he outranks
him. In his haste to pursue Magua, he mistakes the trail
the party must follow and proves utterly incapable of reading the signs of Magua's passage. Natty likens his rash
conduct to that of "babbling women, or eager boys" and
tells him to "keep in our rear, and be careful not to cross
the trail" (188–89).

Cooper reenforces the symmetry of the two halves of
his novel by duplicating in almost exact detail Heyward's
initial dealings with Magua. When Natty identifies a sni-
per who has fired on the party as an Oneida, a tribe allied
with the British, Heyward repeats the error of his first
encounter with the scout. "The poor fellow," he tells Natty, "has mistaken us for French or he would not have
attempted the life of a friend" (196). Natty's efforts to

---

11 The Leatherstocking Tales are, in general, an exercise in rewriting.
Each novel revises and reframes the action of the preceding tales. In *Mohicans*,
the thrust of that process is to confirm the assumptions of *The Pioneers*.
In the later volumes of the series, Cooper reinvokes his earlier writing to
overturn his prior meliorism.

disabuse Heyward of his naïve conception of Indian loyalty are as futile as his earlier insistence that Magua should be killed. Demonstrating the same inappropriate chivalry that permitted Magua to escape, Heyward condemns Natty's willingness to kill any Oneida as "an abuse of our treaties, and unworthy of your character" (196).

When Natty then attempts to avoid a band of Oneida warriors, he must again contend with Heyward's obstinancy. "Our presence," Heyward tells him, "the authority of Colonel Munro would prove a sufficient protection against the anger of our allies . . . I trust, in Heaven, you have not deviated a single foot from the direct line of our course, with so slight a reason" (202). Natty's response further illuminates Heyward's distorted judgment and aligns it with the European blindness which has provoked the William Henry massacre. "Do you think," he asks Heyward, "the bullet of that varlet's rifle would have turned aside, though his sacred majesty the King had stood in its path! . . . Why did not the grand Frencher, he who is captain general of the Canadas, bury the tomahawks of the Hurons, if a word from a white can work such magic on the natur' of an Indian?" (202).

When Heyward's erstwhile allies begin to fire on the party's canoe, he again indulges in the foolish gallantry that marked his conduct at Glenn's Falls. Rejecting Natty's suggestion that he and Munro should take cover in the bottom of the craft, he insists that "it would be but an ill example for the highest in rank to dodge, while the warriors were under fire. . . . All that you say is very true, my friend . . . still our customs must prevent us from doing as you wish" (207). Cooper uses the plural possessive here, and in a number of other incidents in the novel, to clarify the sources of Heyward's identity. Rather than patterning his conduct on Natty, he continues to observe the codes of Europe and offers that model as an "example" for Natty and Chingachgook.

In reproducing the opening chapters of *Mohicans* in this fashion, Cooper returns the novel to the same point of decision he framed just prior to Heyward's and Natty's arrival at William Henry. Once more the fate of his characters and the course of American history depend upon Heyward's ability to redirect his vision. Rather than preserving the deterministic thesis of the first half of *Mohicans*, Cooper alters his narrative course. In a series of climactic episodes, Heyward demonstrates his capacity for growth and achieves a level of autonomy. Instead of advocating a rash assault when the rescuers discover Magua's camp, Heyward volunteers to enter the village as a spy. "You have the means of disguise," he tells Natty, "change me; paint me too, if you will; in short alter me to any thing—a fool" (228). Natty reacts to Duncan's request with "speechless amazement." Not only has Heyward resigned the chivalric conventions which he had maintained at the risk of his life, but he has also abandoned his identity as a Royal American. That decision, Cooper makes quite clear, does not constitute a lapse into savagery. By donning a disguise, Heyward doesn't become an Indian but a civilized version of Natty Bumppo—a character capable of surviving in the wilderness while he preserves the "moral courage" without which, Cooper insists, "no man can be truly great" (180).

Heyward's masquerade is effective. He releases Alice and, with Natty's help, takes her to a Mohican camp where Magua has installed Cora. There, he displays his newly won self-reliance. In Heyward's presence, Magua tells the Mohicans that Natty, whom he describes as an enemy of the tribe, is in their midst. When the Mohicans demand that the scout identify himself, Heyward claims to be "La Longue Carabine," the name the French have given Natty. His intentions are twofold. First, he seeks to save Natty's life by offering his own in its place; and second, he attempts to force Magua's hand in front of the Mohicans. Heyward, then, has become Natty not only by appropriating his name but also by acquiring his cunning. Natty deflects Heyward's ploy by establishing his identity through an exhibition of marksmanship, but Heyward's scheme is successful nonetheless. By delaying Magua's vengeance, he gives Uncas sufficient time to win the trust of his tribesmen and secure Natty's release. Cooper has in this scene effected a thematically significant exchange. Natty has preserved his identity at the potential cost of his life, while Heyward has abandoned his name to rescue his friend.

Cooper extends the implications of this role reversal by imbedding Heyward's disguise in a larger pattern of shifting identities. Natty assists Heyward in releasing Alice by costuming himself as an Indian medicine man disguised as a bear; Uncas escapes imprisonment by assuming Natty's bearskin, while Natty dresses as David Gamut; Chingachgook defends Colonel Munro by masquerading as a beaver. In each of these cases, a willingness to adopt a new identity yields survival and triumph. Heyward's participation in this process is, of course, the most significant aspect of Cooper's motif. By relinquishing the destructive role of a colonial officer, he replaces Natty as *Mohicans'* dominant character and reverses the pattern of decline that dominated the first half of the novel. As Natty's rather than Munro's heir, he is now capable of redeeming the promise of the wilderness.

In *Mohicans'* final chapter Cooper affirms Heyward's cultural paternity and resolves the novel's tensions. The Indian nation has been broken. Uncas, the last hope of his people, and Magua, the firebrand of their potential revolution, have been killed in the novel's final battle. Colonel Munro witnesses the burial of Cora, who has also been slain in the struggle, and is, like Major Effingham, consigned to senility and death. Natty and Chingachgook pledge their brotherhood and retreat to the forest to await the final dispossession of *The Pioneers*. Heyward and Alice seal their engagement and, as the novel's other characters depart, remain as the founders of America's future.

As in *The Pioneers*, Cooper secures the promise implicit in their marriage by describing the contemporary condition of the novel's setting. "There are fashionable and well-attended watering-places," he tells us, "at and near the spring where Hawk-eye halted to drink, and roads traverse the forests where he and his friends were compelled to journey without even a path. Glenn's has a large village; and while William Henry, and even a fortress of later date, are only to be traced as ruins, there is another village on the shore of the Horican" (7). In a later passage, he reports that "the tourist, the valetudinarian, or the amateur of the beauties of nature, in the train of his four-in-hand, now rolls through the scenes we have attempted to describe, in quest of information, health, or pleasure" (147). Within fifty years "the wealth, beauty, and talents, of a hemisphere, were to assemble in throngs," at one of Natty's camp sites to enjoy the virtues of Ballston Spa (123).

In the second half of *Mohicans*, then, Cooper offsets

the skepticism of the novel's preliminary assumptions. History, he now maintains, need not be repetitive; man can escape the determining power of the past. A precursor of the founding fathers of the revolution, Heyward has broken with Europe to launch an independent national destiny.[12] But regardless of the absolute terms in which Cooper describes Heyward's triumph, his historical perspective is no less ambiguous in *Mohicans*' than it was in *The Pioneers*. We are still confronted by two competing paradigms. On one hand, Heyward's conversion advances a resounding defense of American originality—from the destruction of the French and Indian Wars, a new national consciousness has emerged. In Richard Slotkin's terms, regeneration has been achieved through violence.[13] And yet, we are offered, in the first half of *Mohicans*, a static conception of time. Every culture, Cooper suggests, is governed by a cyclic process of growth and decline. America's future will, therefore, necessarily recapitulate the European and the tribal past.

Which half of *Mohicans* represents Cooper's assessment of the form of national time? Unless we are willing to accept Thomas Philbrick's analysis of the novel as a work devoid of "conscious intellectual control," we must assume that Cooper is arguing that at a significant moment, America cast off its dependence on Europe and inaugurated an unprecedented history.[14] But that position is complicated by the role Cooper assigns Natty Bumppo. Natty's rejec-

12 Although Cooper abandoned his projected series of revolutionary war novels to write *Mohicans*, that initiating event of national history significantly informs his narrative.

13 Slotkin, 3–24.

14 Thomas Philbrick, "The Last of the Mohicans and the Sounds of Discord," *American Literature* 36 (May 1964): 209–14.

tion of historically bound codes of conduct establishes him
as the fountainhead of American freedom. By following
his example, Duncan Heyward has secured the nation's
departure from the past. Natty's ability to exempt himself
from human weakness is certainly a consistent feature of
his character. Judge Temple, we recall, argued that Natty
was "an exception," a man for whom the restraints of civil
law were unnecessary. But within the frame of Cooper's
logic in *Mohicans*, Natty is an exception, not in the sense
that his self-control is stronger than that of other men, but
in the sense that he is not a man. By distancing himself
from what Cooper describes as a universal proclivity for
greed and aggression—qualities implicit in the centuries of
Indian and European warfare which inform the novel—
Natty ceases to be a character and becomes an emblem of
unrealizable desire.

   If viewed as an aspect of fictional strategy, that role
is a legitimate one, but Cooper violates the human limitations he has established, first, by transmitting Natty's exceptional status to Duncan Heyward and, then, by suggest-
ing that Heyward will become the progenitor of a race of
exceptions. Cooper's initial argument that Natty's transcendent relation with nature cannot withstand the intrusion
of civilization has been abrogated. The originality Natty
can only enjoy in the pristine wilderness has, in the second
half of *Mohicans*, become a societal hallmark. The development of Heyward's character, on which Cooper predicates
his defense of American primacy, is not the result of a rite
of passage but of a suspension of Cooper's narrative logic.

   Cooper does not directly engage this contradiction but
shifts the grounds of his argument. A stubborn but remedi-
able reliance on convention and not historical necessity be-

comes the source of cultural decline. The tribes collapse because they refuse to abandon their ancient enmities to oppose the European invasion as a unified force. The English and the French armies are destroyed because their leaders are unwilling to adjust their strategies to the circumstances of the frontier. Britain eventually loses its American holdings because it is reluctant to align its colonial policy with progressive developments in North America. The "imbecility" Cooper discovers in European dealings in the New World is the product, we are told, not of organic decay but of particular mistaken decisions. The difficulty here is that Cooper does not link his arguments about the constancy of human nature and the viability of reform. These perspectives operate quite independently in *Mohicans*. We are first invited to adopt a melancholy view of man's aspirations and then are encouraged to celebrate his potential for rebirth and renewal.

There are three ways, I believe, in which we might hope to clarify this narrative confusion. Most obviously, the consistency of Cooper's perspective in *Mohicans* may be defended by arguing that he distinguishes America's history from that of Europe and the tribes solely on the basis of its relative youth. The nation survives the wreck of empire only to reinitiate the temporal cycle which the Indians, the British, and the French have exhausted. Such a viewpoint is consistent with Cooper's ambivalent response to tradition—by describing American history as both a departure from and a repetition of the course of Old World experience, he would blur the polarities which divided his consciousness—but it is disjunctive with the overarching spirit of *Mohicans*. Natty, and ultimately Duncan Heyward, are the heroes of Cooper's novel because they preserve

their difference from the cultures which surround them.
Natty's singularity is axiomatic. He remains a man without a cross who exiles himself from participation in any
community broader than his brotherhood with Chingachgook. Heyward's autonomy would seem to be less certain;
first, because he marries Alice Munro, and second, because
he is closely linked to Uncas. Both of these bonds, however,
illustrate Heyward's distance from Cooper's European and
Indian characters rather than his rapprochement with the
traditions they represent.

Unlike Oliver Effingham's marriage to Elizabeth
Temple, Heyward's union with Alice does not reconcile
two conflicting heritages but emphasizes their rupture.
Colonel Munro's authority has been broken at William
Henry; Heyward succeeds in the second half of the novel
precisely because he repudiates his example and ceases to
be a Royal American. By marrying Alice he frees her not
only from Indian captivity but from her dependence on
her father as well.[15] Cooper directs Heyward's friendship
with Uncas to a similar purpose. Although the two men
are closely aligned during the novel's concluding episodes,
Uncas's death terminates any prospect that he will join
with Heyward to reproduce Natty and Chingachgook's
fraternal bond. Indeed, Cooper rejects the potential of even
a metaphoric racial communion in *Mohicans'* final chapter.
There Munro witnesses the burial of Cora and Uncas and
asks Natty to tell the gathered Indians that "the time shall
not be distant, when we may assemble around his throne
without distinction of sex, or rank, or colour." Natty scorns

15 Heyward's displacement of Colonel Munro's paternal power parallels,
of course, Oliver Effingham's acquisition of Judge Temple's lands and
daughter in *The Pioneers.*

Munro's request and insists that "to tell them this would be to tell them that the snows come not in winter, or that the sun shines fiercest when the trees are stripped of their leaves" (347). Whatever psychosexual purpose Cooper's horror of miscegenation may serve, it functions here to preclude a cultural synthesis of any sort. Heyward is not a mediator like Oliver Effingham but a character whose identity is predicated on his independence from the Mohicans and the Iroquois, the British and the French. Cooper's energies are firmly committed to Heyward's denial of the constituent traditions of the novel. To argue, then, that Cooper undercuts Heyward's hard-won particularity by insisting that America's history will retrace the course of the Old World is to seriously misread his intentions.

A level of narrative coherence might also be achieved by describing the novel's cyclic perception of history as tropological. Shaped by an associationist aesthetic, Cooper's fiction aspires toward images of the sublime, the beautiful, and the picturesque. Lacking the architectural ruins available to European writers, Cooper, as Donald Ringe has argued, employs Tamenund, the conquered tribes, the vanquished imperial armies, and the exiled Natty and Chingachgook as human versions of crumbling manors and battlements.[16] The presence of these characters in *Mohicans*—and Cooper's more general interest in cultural decline—may be regarded not as an indication of historiographic ambivalence but as a contrived effect, a code directed toward a stylistic rather than a thematic end. Certainly there is ample precedent for this convention not only in the proto-romantic art of Europe but in the Knickerbocker school as

16 Donald Ringe, *The Pictorial Mode: Space and Time in the Art of Bryant, Irving, and Cooper* (Lexington, Ky., 1971), 133–38.

well. Asher Durand's coupled paintings *The Morning of Life* and *The Evening of Life*, Thomas Cole's *The Course of Empire*, Washington Irving's *Alhambra* and "Rip Van Winkle" and William Cullen Bryant's poems "The Prairies," "The Indian at the Burial Mound of His Fathers," "The Flood of Years," and "The Ages" parallel Cooper's elegiac intentions in *Mohicans*. Indeed, Cooper's use of ruins as an aesthetic device is not limited to his characterizations or his consideration of cultural decay. His descriptions of the deteriorating blockhouse where Natty and his friends camp during their pursuit of Magua, of the "bloody pond" where Baron Dieskau's troops were defeated by Sir William Johnson, and of the crumbling remains of Fort Oswego provide additional evidence of his evocative objectives.

None of these artists, and here I include Cooper, were as skeptical about progress as their interest in cycle and decline would suggest. They were men living in the country of the future, and if they anticipated the nation's destruction, they did so with no particular sense of urgency or inevitability. Images of human and cultural decay were for them props of a sort, emblems designed to produce a melancholy response from their audience. To confuse these tropes with the world views of their authors is to mistake the painters and writers of the Hudson River School for the romantics. Cooper, Durand, Cole, Irving, and their contemporaries are transitional figures to be sure, but their artistry is more mechanistic and finally more confident than it is spontaneous and world weary.

Dismissing *Mohicans*' cyclic paradigm as a stylistic convention does not, however, resolve the contradiction between Cooper's conceptions of human constancy and American difference but merely relocates it at a further remove. Cooper's reliance on an associationist aesthetic presupposes a universalist perspective inconsistent with his defense of America's liberation from the past. The informing assumption of associationist psychology is the uniformity of human perception and response.[17] The sublime, the beautiful, and the picturesque were defined as stimuli which would yield a constant response. While an image is filtered, the associationists argued, through the viewer's or the reader's own experience, certain topoi—a blasted tree, a cascading waterfall, a bucolic landscape—are common to the experience of all cultivated men and will, when reproduced by the artist, generate an entirely predictable response. Any ruin will, for example, evoke a conception of the vanity of human endeavor, which will, in turn, yield a pleasurable melancholy. By embracing this mechanistic model of human consciousness, Cooper, regardless of the extent of his commitment to a cyclic vision of history, affirms the uniform character of man's consciousness and, hence, the impossibility of American originality.

Finally, Tamenund's projection of national decline may be interpreted as a warning rather than as a statement of historical determinism. *If* America fails to maintain its distance from both savagery and decadence, *then* history will repeat itself. Certainly there is a strongly didactic strain in *Mohicans*. Cooper's demand that his countrymen abandon their reliance on European canons of judgment, which was to become a recurrent theme in his writing, is sounded with particular vigor here. But granting that the cyclic model of *Mohicans* functions as a cautionary emblem does not resolve

17 See Samuel Holt Monk, *The Sublime: A Study of Critical Theories in Eighteenth-Century England* (Ann Arbor, Mich., 1960), and Walter J. Hipple, *The Beautiful, the Sublime, and the Picturesque in Eighteenth-Century British Aesthetic Theory* (Carbondale, Ill., 1957).

the contradictions implicit in the novel's historiographic perspective. Even if Cooper does define America's freedom from the past as a precarious liberation, that perspective is still disjunctive with *Mohicans'* conception of cultural constancy. Moreover, Cooper's argument that the Indians and Europeans of the novel fall because they refuse to adapt their traditions to the circumstances of the frontier is inconsistent with an assumption that America may avoid a similar decline by rigidly adhering to its distinctive principles. If the French and British failure to realize the promise of a new continent results from an unwillingness to relinquish their history, and if the Indians are destroyed because they refuse to deny their traditions and unite against the Europeans, by the terms of Cooper's logic, the preservation of cultural boundaries implies destruction and not redemption. The source of America's freedom from history would then be identical to the cause of the European and Indian enslavement to the erosions of time.

Quite simply, Cooper's contradictory models of American history are beyond resolution. His concluding chapters do not generate a coherent vision but only reenact the fragile balance of *The Pioneers*. Again Cooper holds in stasis mutually exclusive conceptions of national time. His most perceptive critics have recognized the ambivalence of *Mohicans* and, rather than attempting to recover an illusory clarity, have, from a broad range of perspectives, discussed Cooper's conflicting intentions. In what is arguably the most familiar analysis of *Mohicans*, Leslie Fiedler has described the novel's tensions as originating in a deep-seated opposition between id and superego.[18] Focusing

18 Leslie Fiedler, *Love and Death in the American Novel* (New York, 1966), 190–200.

on his treatment of miscegenation in the novel, Fiedler argues that Cooper discharges his repressed desire and latent misogyny by invoking and then denying the prospect of interracial communion. Harry Henderson has rejected Fiedler's Freudian paradigm and advanced a Marxist reading to account for *Mohicans'* inconsistencies.[19] Cooper employs, Henderson maintains, the destruction of the Mohicans as metaphor for the decline of the gentry in American life—an event which compromised his own social position. Cooper's nationalistic affirmation of America's departure from the past is, from Henderson's perspective, complicated by a sense of his own displacement. Joel Porte attributes *Mohicans'* duality to Cooper's "deep yearning to unite in himself the best qualities of the white man and the *beau ideal* of the redskin."[20] Henry Nash Smith discovers in *Mohicans'* narrative Cooper's simultaneous attraction to the freedom of the wilderness and the order of civilization.[21] H. Daniel Peck, who approaches *Mohicans* from a Bachelardian orientation, has proposed yet another source for the novel's ambiguities. Peck reads *Mohicans* as a doubled work in which "the polar regions of Cooper's imaginative geography" both find expression. *Mohicans* progresses, Peck argues, from reality to dream, from a "landscape of difficulty" to a "region of mythic quest."[22]

At the risk of adopting the excesses of both subjective and logocentric criticism, I would argue that although each of these analyses engages one aspect of Cooper's discourse,

19 Harry Henderson, *Versions of the Past: The Historical Imagination in American Fiction* (New York, 1974), 50–90.

20 Joel Porte, *The Romance in America: Studies in Cooper, Poe, Hawthorne, Melville, and James* (Middletown, Conn., 1969), 39–41.

21 Smith, 64–76.

22 Peck, 120–21.

none of them fully addresses the historiographic concerns
that are at the heart of *Mohicans*' action. Cooper's efforts
to define the shape of national time are, as they were in
The Pioneers, complicated by contradictory imperatives of
both a general and a particular character. Conceived in the
broadest of ways, *Mohicans*' ambivalent conception of the
American past restates what I have described as a recurrent
national attraction to both an Adamic and a progressive
model of history. The elegiac spirit of *Mohicans*, implicit in
Cooper's descriptions of Indian and European decline, affirms America's independence from the weight of history
and locates the source of the culture's originality in the
Armageddon of William Henry. *Mohicans*' cyclic paradigm, in turn, counters the anarchic potential of that
imagined liberation by imposing a more certain and less
vertiginous pattern on the course of national development.
Within the parameters of that historiographic scheme,
America's future is not without direction or precedent.
Whatever anxiety its eventual decline may provoke is alleviated by Cooper's assumption that the young republic
is far removed from the decay of old age.

More specifically, *Mohicans*' structural dichotomy
reflects the paradoxical pressures of Cooper's immediate
context. Like *The Pioneers*, *Mohicans* records a degree of
generational anxiety. Cooper's displacement of the novel's
father figures and his celebration of Duncan Heyward's
ascendancy are further examples of his struggle to resist
the authority of William Cooper and the revolutionary
generation. Simultaneously, the organic metaphor he uses
to describe the trajectory of every culture deflects the fear
of leveling democracy inherent in that rebellion. History,
Cooper suggests, is not chaotic but ordered. Duncan Hey-

ward's paternity will not be threatened until the life of American culture has run its course.

Mohicans does not, however, only recapitulate the social concerns of *The Pioneers*. Cooper was at the time of *Mohicans*' composition far more confident of his literary abilities. No longer the failed son of a successful father, Cooper was now among the most prominent American writers of his day. Preparing as he wrote *Mohicans* for an extended tour of Europe, Cooper adopts in this novel the posture of a national rather than a generational spokesman.[23] Self-conscious of that role, he devotes his narrative energies to a defense of American autonomy, a cause he advances along two primary lines. Most obviously, Cooper assumes a militantly didactic stance. Duncan Heyward's progress from dependence to self-reliance is clearly a parable directed toward a nation far too willing, from Cooper's point of view, to subject itself to the tyranny of European opinion. More important, Cooper attempts to validate America's cultural independence by establishing in *Mohicans* the particularity of its origins. By predicating his novel's narrative progress on Heyward's rejection of European convention, Cooper defines a point of historical rupture.

And yet, demonstrating his culture's difference was inadequate to Cooper's chauvinistic purpose. European critics of American society were themselves prepared to grant the nation's specificity. Indeed their condescension was supported by their sense of America's divergence from accepted standards of social and political decorum. If Cooper was to discharge successfully the role of national spokesman, he must in *Mohicans* establish both America's

23 See Dekker's discussion of Cooper's "pious and patriotic" purposes in *Mohicans*, 64–66.

independence from European history and its cultural
equality. In attempting to realize that latter objective,
Cooper appropriates the cyclic vision of European historians to align American history with the course of prior
empires. His account of the decline and fall of the Indian
and European nations is directed not simply toward the
identification of a point of national origin—a wedge against
the forced continuity of time—but also toward the establishment of America's unity with other cultures whose greatness was built on the ruins of their predecessors. However
disjunctive Cooper's simultaneous use of the William
Henry Massacre to suggest both difference and repetition
remains, this duality reflects a coherent purpose—the defense of the American nation as a culture both separate
and equal.

The paradoxical character of that historiographic strategy is most apparent in Cooper's extensive use of literary
references. In this, the most allusive of his novels, Cooper
invokes, among other sources, Shakespearean drama, the
Waverley Novels, *Paradise Lost*, romantic poetry, and
the epics of Greece and Rome. He does not disguise his
indebtedness but freely admits his borrowings in a series
of epigraphs which align the action of *Mohicans* with the
masterworks he cites. Magua's eloquent defense of his quest
for vengeance is, for example, informed by passages drawn
from *The Merchant of Venice*. His call for an Indian
rebellion follows from an allusion to Milton's Satan.
Munro's anguish at the loss of his daughters is subsumed
by a quotation from *Lear*; the rugged terrain of the American wilderness is glossed by a descriptive passage from
Childe Harold. A Midsummer Night's Dream is a source
for both the novel's forest adventures and its recurrent

pattern of disguise and shifting identities. Scott's wavering heroes are acknowledged as the models on which Heyward's character is founded. Natty's adventures are associated with those of the epic heroes of *The Odyssey*, *The Iliad*, and *The Aeneid*. Cooper turns to the graveyard poetry of Thomas Gray as a context for the forests' ghostly shades and to the *Henry* plays as referents for the shifting political tides of the novel. In each of these incidents, and in many other episodes in *Mohicans*, Cooper insistently locates his writing within the European literary tradition.

Cooper's conscious display of his reading is neither an act of submission nor an attempt to announce his sophistication but is, rather, a declaration of national primacy. Because American history has generated, he implies, a narrative which replicates the form and the action of the most fundamental documents of the European tradition, its cultural authority is no less certain than that of Britain, Rome, or Greece. Cooper's strategy is by no means unique. It parallels the national demand for an American epic which had been sounded since the eighteenth century and which had provoked some of the worst poetry of the Federalist period.[24] Implicit in that call was the assumption that if America were to take its rightful place with the great empires of world history, it must produce an *Odyssey*, an *Aeneid*, or a *Paradise Lost* of its own. In other words, cultural independence required duplication. Cooper's sensitivity to this imagined national need is most clearly manifested in *Lionel Lincoln*, the novel which immediately preceeds *Mohicans* in Cooper's canon. *Lionel Lincoln*, as I have noted, was to have been the first volume of a thirteen-

24 See Gregory Payne's discussion of that crusade in "Cooper and *The North American Review*," *Studies in Philology* 28 (1931): 267–77.

novel history of the original colonies. Cooper conceived that project not as a series of local chronicles but as a prose epic which would record the emergence of an American character and vision.[25] He did not abandon that intention with the commercial failure of *Lionel Lincoln*, but in *Mohicans* conflates thirteen novels into one to celebrate his nation's heroic tradition.[26]

Cooper's reliance on European literary models to dispute their inhibiting power is, of course, as paradoxical as the historical perspective he advances in *Mohicans*. He incorporates a cyclic vision of history in the novel not in the interests of a deterministic world view but as a narrative ploy designed to establish both difference and equality. The inconsistent logic that results from that effort illustrates the conflicting objectives American writers necessarily confronted in their attempts to impose form on national experience. In *Mohicans* Cooper remains a victim of that dilemma, a writer bound by a conflict he was unable to resolve.

25 For discussions of this projected series, see Dekker, 64, and John P. McWilliams, Jr., *Political Justice in a Republic: James Fenimore Cooper's America* (Berkeley, 1972), 84.

26 *Mohicans*' epic aspects are noted in Charles A. Brady, "Myth-Maker and Christian Romancer," in *American Classics Reconsidered*, ed. Harold Gardiner, S. J. (New York, 1958); Donald Darnell, "Uncas as Hero: The Ubi Sunt Formula in *The Last of the Mohicans*," *American Literature* 37 (November 1965): 259–66; Fiedler, 188–92; Porte, 39–41.

3

Containing American History: *The Prairie* and the New West

Formally, the mind wants to conceive a point in either time or space that marks the beginning of all things (or at least of a limited set of central things), but like Oedipus the mind risks discovering, at that point, where all things will end as well. Underlying this formal quest is an imaginative and emotional need for unity, a need to apprehend an otherwise dispersed number of circumstances and to put them in some sort of telling order, sequential, moral, or logical.

—*Edward Said*, Beginnings

But from these immense prairies may arise one great advantage to the United States, viz: The restriction of our population to some certain limits, and therby a continuation of the Union. Our citizens being so prone to rambling and extending themselves on the frontiers will, through necessity, be constrained to limit their extent in the west to the borders of the Missouri and Mississippi, while they leave the prairies incapable of cultivation to the wandering and uncivilized aborigines of the country.

—The Expeditions of Zebulon Montgomery Pike

ONE of Cooper's primary concerns in both *The Pioneers* and *The Last of the Mohicans* is the location of a cultural genesis. By designating points of national departure, he erects a fictive barrier against the past and validates his claims for American "originality." Cooper does not, however, simply privilege a moment in time from which the course of national development has followed but conceives beginnings which also imply endings. In *The Pioneers*, Judge Temple's arrival in the forests of New York launches a distinctive cultural destiny, but that origin is not self-contained. It requires the ascendancy of Oliver Effingham —a transition which fixes the direction of national history— for its completion. Similarly, in *Mohicans* Cooper discovers in the carnage of William Henry a source for American particularity, but he depends upon the marriage of Duncan Heyward and Alice Munro to fulfill and to contain the process of beginning which the massacre initiates. The origins which Cooper identifies in these novels are not, in other words, discrete events but temporal brackets which suggest the totality of the nation's formative experience.[1] Cooper has, then, in the first two Leatherstocking Tales, disarmed both the intrusive power of the past and the revisionary potential of the future. He gains thereby a resultant mastery of time and becomes, quite literally, the author of his culture. Because his beginnings are closed temporal circuits, America's origins, as Cooper imagines them in these novels, are at once the source of rupture and continuity, of freedom and restraint.

    And yet, the authority of Cooper's historical perspective in *The Pioneers* and *Mohicans* is not self-sufficient but is predicated upon our willingness to accord his characters the emblematic status he assigns them. As I have argued, that concession is problematic. We may believe that Oliver

1 Cooper does extend his historical surveys beyond the frame he constructs. *The Pioneers* and *Mohicans* look back in time to the pristine wilderness and forward to the contemporary condition of their settings. But all that precedes the inaugural action of these tales is merely overture, the residue of colonial history. The subsequent expansion of American civilization is, in turn, only the certain consequence of the respective achievements of Oliver Effingham and Duncan Heyward.

Effingham is capable of promoting the development of Templeton, but Cooper demands from us a more extensive commitment to his potency. If *The Pioneers'* historical perspective is to remain credible, we must perceive Effingham as a representative man whose displacement of Judge Temple guarantees the progressive course of the nation as a whole. Despite his attractive qualities, Effingham is incapable of bearing that metaphoric burden. Cooper fails to demonstrate his ability to defuse the latent tensions of the novel and relies instead on his description of contemporary New York to document Effingham's enduring influence. Duncan Heyward's repudiation of European convention is also somewhat persuasive on the level of character, but again Cooper is not content to deal with the particular. When he generalizes Heyward's achievement and identifies him as the figurative progenitor of a race of exceptions, his argument becomes mired in paradox. The accomplishments of Oliver Effingham and Duncan Heyward are, in short, plausible enough within the novels in which they appear, but neither of these characters convincingly illustrates the emergence of a class resistant to historical change. Like the heroes of the Waverley Novels, Effingham and Heyward are representative men in the sense that they are the products of their times, but Cooper departs from Scott's model to argue that his young heroes are determining as well as determined characters. This extension of their narrative function is not fully supported and is ultimately fatal for Cooper's historiographic intentions.

In *The Prairie* (1827), the third volume of the Leatherstocking Tales, Cooper evades this narrative difficulty by abandoning metaphor for abstraction. Rather than bracketing an arbitrary period of American time to suggest the range of national experience, he engages the absolute limits of that history. Although *The Prairie*, which is set in 1805, describes a period of American life posterior to the events of *The Pioneers* and *Mohicans*, the point of cultural origin Cooper defines in this novel is considerably more remote than those of the first two Tales. His central characters, the Bush family, are nomadic squatters, precursors of the settlers of Templeton and the European and colonial officers of *Mohicans*. Their patriarchal government predates the more complex social order of Templeton; their perspective is uninformed by the restrictive heritage which shapes the conduct of *Mohicans*' characters. Unlike the forests of the first two Tales, which bear the marks of prior events, the Great Plains—against which *The Prairie*'s adventures unfold—is a black slate, devoid of "historical recollections."[2] Only a few trappers and explorers have penetrated its boundaries. The Pawnee and Sioux, who hunt the buffalo there, are roving bands whose encampments are transitory. When, in the novel's opening scene, Ishmael Bush leads his clan across the Mississippi and into the prairie's vacant landscape, we stand at the very beginnings of cultural life.[3]

The primal origin which Cooper invokes in *The Prairie* is balanced by an equally absolute sense of an ending. The first two volumes of the Tales looked forward to the west-

---

2 James Fenimore Cooper, *The Prairie*, Darley-Townscend edition (New York, 1859), 17. Future references will be to this edition and will be cited by page number in the text.

3 See William Wasserstrom's consideration of the Bush family as characters who suggest a primal state of social being in "Cooper, Freud, and the Origins of Culture," *American Imago* 17 (1960): 423–37.

ern advance of American settlement. Natty's role in these novels, as Cooper describes it in *The Pioneers,* is that of an advance guard, "the foremost of that band of pioneers who are opening the way for the march of the nation across the continent."[4] The "thriving villages" and "valetudinarian" retreats which grace the contemporary settings of *The Pioneers* and *Mohicans* testify to the success of that progressive process. But in *The Prairie,* Cooper neither affirms nor anticipates such development. Although he does note the formation of communities in the trans-Mississippi West and accords a "magical rapidity to settlement there," he observes that "by far the greater portion" of western immigrants have established "themselves along the margins of the larger water-courses" and have not pressed beyond the riverbanks into the plains (11).

Even as he celebrates the wisdom of the Louisiana Purchase, Cooper does not envision the settlement of that newly acquired territory. The Mississippi's western bank will, he predicts, provide America with "a belt of fertile country," but nature has "placed a barrier of desert to the extension of our population in the West" (9).[5] The advantages of the Purchase proceed for Cooper not from the prospect of unlimited western expansion but from the exclusion of alien powers from America's boundary and from the control of trade routes in the nation's interior. Indeed, rather than imagining "the march of the nation across the continent," Cooper foresees a "peaceful division of this vast empire" through which a new nation "friendly to the inter-

4 *The Pioneers,* 456.
5 See Smith's discussion of the Great American Desert in *Virgin Land,* 174–83.

ests of the United States" will be forged into the Louisiana territories (9).[6] Significantly, none of the white characters of *The Prairie* remain in the grasslands to initiate the process of civilization but return to the Mississippi to pursue their destinies within the more settled areas of the American West. The Great Plains prove to be inhospitable territory unsuited even to the primitive needs of the Bush family. Cooper's characters turn their backs to the frontier; the nation's westward movement has come to an end.

Cooper's extension of his historical frame to the absolute beginning and end of American development is reenforced by the relationship he establishes between *The Prairie* and the first two volumes of the Tales. Cooper did not anticipate his return to the series in *The Pathfinder* and *The Deerslayer* and assumed that *The Prairie* would conclude his saga.[7] With that sense of closure in mind, he recalls, through Natty's reminiscence, the major events of the first two Tales, places them in chronological order, and completes the series by describing Natty's death. This process of summary and conclusion is, Cooper tells us in his preface, a major concern of the novel. "It is quote probable," he writes,

> that the narrator of these simple events has deceived himself as to the importance they may have in the eyes of other people.

6 This projection of the rise of a new nation in the trans-Mississippi West is disjunctive with Cooper's insistence that the Plains will serve as a barrier to future settlement, a contradiction which suggests the precarious quality of Cooper's confidence in national closure.

7 In his preface to *The Prairie*, for example, Cooper remarks that "this book closes the career of Leatherstocking." When he returned to the series thirteen years later in *The Pathfinder*, he described Natty as a character who had "been regularly consigned to his grave." See, too, *L&J* 1:167, 168, and Terence Martin's essay "Beginnings and Endings in the Leatherstocking Tales," *Nineteenth-Century Fiction* 33 (June 1978): 69–87.

But he has seen, or thought he has seen, something sufficiently instructive and touching in the life of a veteran of the forest, who having commenced his career near the Atlantic, had been drawn by the increasing and unparalleled advance of population to seek a final refuge against society in the broad and tenantless plains of the west, to induce him to hazard the experiment of publication. That the changes which might have drawn a man so constituted to such a single life, is a matter of undeniable history; that they did produce such an effect on the Scout of *Mohicans*, the Leatherstocking of the *Pioneers* and the Trapper of the *Prairie* rests on an authority no less imposing than these veritable pages from which the reader shall no longer be detained.

Natty's life, Cooper maintains, epitomizes the history of the American people. By tracing the course of his adventures, as he does in *The Prairie*, he recovers the totality of national experience and contains it within the scope of his narrative. Less an historical novel than a metahistorical romance, *The Prairie* is a work of self-conscious review. It is the capstone not only of Natty's career and of the first three volumes of the Leatherstocking Tales but also of Cooper's investigation of New World experience.[8]

The metahistorical objectives of *The Prairie* are apparent in Cooper's narrative design and in his approach to characterization as well as in the abstracted quality of his temporal frame. *The Prairie*'s plot, which George Dekker has described as "the feeblest and most mechanical narra-

---

8 Although Cooper based some of his characters, incidents, and settings on contemporary accounts of the New West—most particularly those of the Lewis and Clark and the Long expeditions—*The Prairie* is primarily the product of invention. Unlike *The Pioneers* which is predicated on Cooper's boyhood experience, and unlike *Mohicans* which is based on historical incident, *The Prairie* has its source not in fact but in a theoretical conception of cultural evolution.

tive in the Leatherstocking series," is byzantine.[9] Ishmael Bush and his family are in flight from the law both as the suspected murderers of a deputy sheriff and as the kidnappers of Inez de Certavallos, a Spanish heiress. They are followed by Paul Hover, a yeoman bee hunter who is in love with Bush's niece Ellen Wade, and by Inez's husband, Capt. Duncan Uncas Middleton, the grandson of Duncan Heyward and the namesake of Chingachgook's son. In the course of that pursuit, the Bush family, Hover, and Middleton encounter Natty, who appears in this novel as an eighty-six-year-old trapper; Obed Bat, an eastern naturalist who has come to the prairie in search of new species of plant and animal life; and two bands of plains' Indians, the Pawnee and the Sioux. The novel's subsequent action centers on Ishmael's attempts to reclaim his stolen cattle from the Sioux and on Hover's and Middleton's efforts to release Ellen and Inez from Ishmael's control. The conjunction of these disparate characters in the unsettled space of the plains severely strains *The Prairie*'s credibility. Cooper himself came to regret the range of his characterization and argued that the novel would have been more effective had he limited his scope to the Bush family, Natty, and the Sioux and Pawnee tribesmen—characters whose presence in the Plains might be convincingly established.[10] His interests in writing *The Prairie*, however, are not directed primarily toward fictive coherence or plausibility but toward a comprehensive survey of the variety of American experience.

9 Dekker, 101. For opposing perspectives which defend the narrative coherence of *The Prairie*, see Smith, 256–60, and Richard Chase, *The American Novel and Its Tradition* (New York, 1957), 52–65.

10 Susan F. Cooper, 157.

Cooper announces that intention very early in the novel when he remarks that

> the march of civilization with us, has a strong analogy to that of all coming events, which are known to cast their shadows before. The gradations of society, from that state which is called refined to that which approaches as near barbarity as connexion with an intelligent people will readily allow, are to be traced from the bosom of the states, where wealth, luxury and the arts are beginning to seat themselves, to those distant, and ever-receding borders which mark the skirts and announce the approach of the nation, as morning mists precede the signs of day. [79]

He then illustrates that evolutionary process by assembling in *The Prairie* types of each of these "gradations of society." Ishmael Bush is, for example, not merely a restless nomad, but as his name suggests, he is the quintessential squatter, the personification of what Kay Seymour House has called "the great American nightmare of the early nineteenth century."[11] A man of "prodigious power" and the "terrible strength of the elephant," he crosses the prairie "in the same sluggish manner [of] an overfatted beast." The "inferior lineaments of his countenance," Cooper observes, "were coarse, extended, and vacant; while the superior, or those nobler points which are thought to affect the intelligent being, were low, receding, and mean" (13).

Bush recognizes no authority but his own and has a mortal hatred of the law. "I have come into these districts," he tells Natty, "because I have found the law sitting too tight upon me, and am not over fond of neighbors who can't

11 Kay Seymour House, *Cooper's Americans* (Columbus, Ohio, 1965), 298.

settle a dispute without troubling a justice and twelve men"
(73). He boasts "that he had never dwelt where he might
not safely fell every tree he could view from his own
threshold; that the law had rarely been known to enter his
clearing; and that his ears had never willingly admitted
the sound of a church bell" (80). His primary assumption
is "the rule that the 'arth is common property." The "air,
the water, and the ground, are free gifts to man," he argues,
"and no one has the power to portion them out in parcels"
(96). Bush's family is as harrowing as their patriarch. His
sons have inherited his strength and his anarchic proclivi-
ties. His wife, Esther, whom Cooper calls "the Amazon,"
is a thoroughly imposing figure capable of defending the
family's interests against any threat. Even Ishmael's young-
est children recoil from the very word "law" and prompt
Natty to exclaim that "it is a solemn sight to witness how
much human natur' is inclined to evil, in one so young"
(192).

The Bush family's conduct is congruent with their manners and their principles. Ishmael appears in *The Prairie*'s
initial scene with "a keen and bright woodaxe across his
shoulder"—an extravagant gesture in the context of the
virtually treeless Plains. Cooper nevertheless invokes a
stand of cottonwood which Bush and his sons summarily
level. Cooper stresses the violence and the horror implicit
in that act by personifying the trees Ishmael destroys. "At
length," he writes

> the eldest of the sons stepped heavily forward, and without any
> apparent effort, he buried his axe to the eye in the soft body of a
> cotton-wood tree. He stood a moment regarding the effect of
> the blow, with that sort of contempt with which a giant might
> be supposed to contemplate the resistance of a dwarf, and then

flourishing the implement above his head, with the grace and dexterity with which a master of the art of offence would wield his nobler though less useful weapon, he quickly severed the tree, bringing its tall top crashing to the earth, in submission to his prowess. His companions regarded the operation with indolent curiosity, until they saw the prostrate trunk stretched on the ground, when, as if a signal for a general attack had been given, they advanced in a body to the work: and in a space of time, and with a neatness of execution, that would have astonished an ignorant spectator, they stripped a small but suitable spot of its burden of forest, as effectually, and almost as promptly, as if a whirlwind has passed along the place. [21]

The subsequent adventures of the Bush family advance this initial image of their fearsome and lawless potency. Robbed of their cattle by the marauding Sioux, they set off on foot to recover their livestock. More than an equal match for their savage adversaries, they forge an alliance with the Sioux, and when the Indians refuse to return their property, route the mounted tribesmen and reclaim their possessions. Natty, Middleton, and Hover are similarly powerless against the will of Ishmael Bush. They do release Inez and Ellen while Bush is away from his camp, but they are unable to prevail against his strength. Ishmael reverses the novel's pursuit, recaptures the women, and imprisons their rescuers. Having deflected every challenge to his authority, he then determines the fate of Cooper's other characters.

My point is not that Ishmael and his family are ideas clumsily masquerading as characters—Ishmael himself is one of Cooper's most memorable creations—but, rather, that they are the embodiment of two centuries of American anxiety about the frontier. Despite Cooper's assertion that "there was little" in the appearance of the Bush family "that is not daily to be encountered on the highways of our changeable and moving country," they are not figures drawn from life but characters modeled on the hostile borderers of Cotton Mather, William Byrd, Timothy Dwight, Hugh Henry Brackenridge, Edwin James, and many other American writers who associated the nation's western boundary with disruption and potential chaos (14).[12] Their massive strength and frightening lawlessness are the generalized expression of their class, resonant elements of an American iconography.

As much as the Bush family are the stylized projections of the initial stage of cultural development, Inez de Certavallos is an idealized image of the outer limit of that process. Unlike Major Effingham and Colonel Munro, who transmit the values of the Old World in *The Pioneers* and *Mohicans*, Inez is not a child of England but of Spain. Certainly, Cooper perceived the context Effingham and Munro represent as a repressive force capable of inhibiting American progress, but the historical burden implicit in Inez's heritage is more highly charged. An heir of the Spanish Inquisition and autocratic rule, she is an emblem not only of historical inscription but also of absolute despotism and cultural decadence.

Cooper establishes Inez's representative status by describing her as the inverse of Esther Bush, a diminutive model of civilized womanhood. "Her person," he observes, "was of the smallest size that is believed to comport with

12 Cooper abstracts the Bush family in much the same way that he extends his conception of beginnings and endings. In *The Pioneers*, the restless borderer is typified by Jotham Riddel, a man who exchanged his property on a seasonal basis. Cooper undoubtedly intended Riddel to serve as an emblem of social chaos, but he achieved that effect by describing him as an average member of his class. In *The Prairie*, Cooper abandons his interest in the social mean to craft figures who suggest collective extremes.

beauty, and which poets and artists have chosen as the *beau ideal* of female loveliness" (111). Her presence in *The Prairie* is barely corporeal. Kept like a sacred talisman in a tent mounted on one of Bush's wagons, her first appearance in the novel produces "astonishment" and "profound silence." Bush's sons gaze on her as if she were "some supernatural vision" or "extraordinary . . . spectacle." She is, in Cooper's terms, a "silent wonder" who occupies a realm of experience remote from that of her captors (112).

Cooper's association of Inez with religious imagery is certainly intentional, for the context she suggests is not simply that of the Old World but that of Catholicism. When Middleton meets her in New Orleans, her religion becomes an immediate obstacle to his courtship. Having declared his interest in Inez, he is assigned to the tutelage of Father Ignatius who struggles "to convert him to the true faith." The Jesuit's efforts, which Cooper describes as "systematic, vigorous, and long sustained," are fruitless. Middleton continues to oppose "common sense" and a "little knowledge of the habits of his country" to Ignatius's sophistry (197). Unwilling, however, to admit his failure to Inez's father, Don Augustin, the priest "by a species of pious fraud . . . declared that while no positive change was actually wrought in the mind of Middleton, there was every reason to hope the entering wedge of argument has been driven to its head, and that in consequence an opening was left through which it might rationally be hoped, the blessed seeds of a religious fructification would find their way, especially if the subject was left uninterruptedly to enjoy the advantage of Catholic communion" (198). Don Augustin is convinced by the priest's assurances and grants Middleton his daughter's hand in the full expectation that she will prove "to be a humble instrument of bringing her lover into the bosom of the true church" (198). Inez forwards that intention by asking Middleton on their wedding day to "Be like him in *every* thing. Imitate my father, Middleton, and I can ask no more of you" (200).

Clearly, Cooper identifies Inez and her cultural heritage as a threat to Middleton, who, as the grandson of Duncan Heyward, bears the responsibility of cultural leadership. Catholicism represented for Cooper, as it did for his contemporaries, the full force of European absolutism.[13] Its authoritarian character and insistence on blind faith stood in diametric opposition to America's commitment to the liberty of thought and the integrity of private judgment. Cooper emphasizes the repressive spirit of the Church by describing Father Ignatius's efforts to insulate his community against the arrival of American officers in the Louisiana territories.

> The reckless freedom of such among them as thought only of this life, and the consistent and tempered piety of others, caused the honest priest to look about him in concern. The influence of example on one hand, and the contamination of too free an intercourse on the other, began to manifest themselves even in that portion of his own flock which he had supposed to be too thoroughly folded in spiritual government ever to stray. It was time to turn his thoughts from the offensive, and to prepare his followers to resist the lawless deluge of opinion which threatened to break down the barriers of their faith. Like a wise commander who finds he has occupied too much ground for the amount of his force, he began to curtail his outworks. The relics were concealed from profane eyes; his people were admonished not to speak of miracles before a race that not only

13 See David Levin's discussion of America's association of Catholicism with totalitarian rule in *History as Romantic Art* (Stanford, 1959), 93–125.

denied their existence, but who had even the desperate hardihood to challenge their proofs; and even the Bible itself was once more prohibited with terrible denunciatons, for the triumphant reason that it was liable to be misinterpreted. [198]

The danger Inez poses for Middleton does not involve religious conversion. Cooper no more anticipates the revival of Catholicism in America than he foresees the return of European hegemony. His concern is directed toward the potential decay of democratic government. As ominous as the leveling impulses of the Bush family, the subservience Cooper associates with Inez suggests the betrayal of national principles and the duplication of Old World tyranny. Inez's religion becomes in *The Prairie* a symbol of the oligarchic restraint of progress, the imprisonment of the present by the past. The opposite pole of the continuum the Bush family begins, she is as frightening an image of an American future as are Ishmael and his primal horde.

Having established this diametric opposition between a stage of civilization which admits no restraints and one which permits no liberty, Cooper locates Middleton and Natty between these extremes. Again he emphasizes the representative quality of his characters by casting them as archetypal mediators. Middleton's name is itself an acknowledgment of his role as a figure of compromise. His links to Heyward and Uncas, the moderating figures of *Mohicans*, further identify his function in the novel. But Cooper does not limit his signaling efforts to these allusions. In describing the collision of Spanish and American culture in Louisiana, he explicitly defines the symbolic character of Middleton's marriage to Inez.

In such a novel intermixture, however, of men born and nur-
tured in freedom, and the compliant minions of absolute power,
the catholic and the protestant, the active and the indolent,
some little time was necessary to blend the discrepant elements
of society. In attaining so desirable an end, woman was made
to perform her accustomed and grateful office. The barriers of
prejudice and religion were broken through by the irresistable
power of the master-passion: and family unions, ere long,
began to cement the political tie which had made a forced conjunction between people so opposite in their habits, their educa-
tions, and their opinions. [194]

"Middleton," Cooper concludes, "was among the first of
the new possessors of soil, who became captive to the charms
of a Louisiana lady." The climactic marriages of *The
Pioneers* and *Mohicans* are directed, of course, toward a
similar thematic purpose, but they are metaphors whose
emblematic function is implied rather than announced.

Natty both anticipates and parallels Middleton's dialectical function in *The Prairie*. He shares Ishmael Bush's
regard for personal liberty but, at the same time, supports
the discipline of Spanish Catholicism. As a figure simultaneously committed to freedom and restraint, he suggests
the process of cultural synthesis which Middleton's marriage achieves. Although Natty's role in *The Prairie* is similar to those he enacted in *The Pioneers* and *Mohicans*, his
character has undergone a transformation. That change is
most apparent in the tempering of his perspective. No longer a hunter or an Indian scout, he is now a subsistence trapper. "At my time of life," he tells Ishmael, "food and
clothing be all that is needed; and I have little occasion
for what you call plunder, unless it may be now and then to
barter for a horn of powder or a bar of lead" (26). Resignation and humility have become the hallmarks of his

identity. He dismisses as "vain boasting" accounts of his former adventures and maintains that "it is not with me now as it used to be some forty years ago, when warfare and bloodshed were my calling and my gifts" (238). He has, he says, "seen too much mortal blood poured out in empty quarrels to wish ever to hear an angry rifle again. Ten weary years have I sojourned alone on these naked plains, waiting for my hour, and not a blow have I struck a'gin an enemy more humanized than the grizzly bear" (96).

When Hover advocates a skirmish with the Sioux, in terms which recall Natty's own language in *Mohicans*, Bumppo rejects that plan as "rash and heady." The "day has been, boy," he tells Hover, "when my blood was like your own, too swift and too hot to run quietly in my veins. But what will it profit to talk of silly risks and foolish acts at this time of life? A grey head should cover a brain of reason, and not the tongue of a boaster" (51). Even the claims of self-defense are inadequate to prompt Natty to resume his violent ways. "Blood is not to be spilt to save the life of one so useless and so near his allotted time," he remarks when a stranger approaches his camp. "Let him come on; my skins, my traps, and even my rifle shall be his, if he sees fit to demand them" (34).

Natty's attitude toward civil law has also changed. He still refers to settlements as "abominations" and recalls with undiminished rancour his imprisonment in the stocks of Templeton, but he insists nonetheless that civil authority "is needed when such as have not the gifts of strength and wisdom are to be taken care of" (31). The law, he tells Ellen Wade, is "a friend . . . always bound to look to the young and feeble like yourself." More significant, in one

of the novel's concluding episodes, Natty counsels Paul
Hover to abandon the solitary life of the wilderness for the
comforts and security of the settlements. "Come hither
lad," he tells Hover,

> Much has passed atween us on the pleasures and respectable-
> ness of a life in the woods or on the border. I do not now mean
> to say that all you have heard is not true; but different tempers
> call for different employments. You have taken to your bosom,
> there, a good and kind child, and it has become your duty to
> consider her, as well as yourself, in setting forth in life. You
> are a little given to skirting the settlements; but to my poor
> judgement the girl would be more like a flourishing flower in
> the sun of a clearing, than in the winds of a prairie. Therefore
> forget anything you may have heard from me, which is never-
> theless true, and turn your mind on the ways of the inner
> country. [463]

The transformation of Natty's character is attributable,
to some degree, to old age, but Natty speaks not simply as
a man approaching death but as a kind of frontier mystic.[14]
From his first appearance in the novel to his death in *The
Prairie*'s final pages, Natty is a character who has tran-
scended his mortality. The passage in which Cooper introduces the trapper is certainly the most quoted paragraph
in his canon, but it bears repetition here:

> The sun had fallen below the crest of the nearest wave of the
> prairie, leaving the usual rich and glowing train on its track.
> In the centre of this flood of firey light a human form appeared,
> drawn against the gilded background as distinctly, and seem-

14 A similar perspective is advanced by Marius Bewley in *The Eccentric
Design: Form in the Classic American Novel* (New York, 1970), p. 112;
by Donald Ringe in "Chiaroscuro as an Artistic Device in Cooper's Fiction,"
PMLA 78 (1963): 350–51; and by Joel Porte in *Romance in America*,
42–44.

ingly as palpable, as though it would come within the grasp of any extended hand. The figure was colossal; the attitude musing and melancholy; and the situation directly in route of the travellers. But, imbedded, as it was, in its settings of garish light, it was impossible to distinguish more concerning its proportions or true character. [16]

Although Cooper explains Natty's distorted scale in this scene as an optical illusion, he continues to stress his superhuman status throughout the novel. When Hover first encounters the trapper, he asks him, "From what cloud have you fallen, my good old man?" Natty's response— "I have been long on earth, and never I hope nigher to heaven than I am at this moment"—establishes not just his advanced age but his impending sainthood (35).

Natty is not, as he was in *The Pioneers* and *Mohicans*, a partisan of any cause. He is "strictly neutral" in the conflicts of the novel and remains largely indifferent to its characters' private concerns and struggles (97). He advances assistance when it is asked and willingly offers his own life to preserve those of his companions, but his interests are not those of mortal men. Profit, comfort, conquest, and even survival have no appeal for Natty in *The Prairie*. He has acquired a superior perspective that leads him to dismiss human endeavor as vanity. "What is life and what is death," he asks Obed Bat. "Your l'arning, though it is man's boast, is folly in the eyes of Him who sits in the clouds, and looks down in sorrow at the pride and vanity of his creatur's" (224).

In rhetoric reminiscent of Natty's initial appearance in the novel, Cooper describes his death as an apotheosis. As Middleton watches over Natty's final hours, he imagines that "he could read the workings of the old man's soul in

the strong lineaments of his countenance." Cooper acknowledges that Middleton's vision of Natty's transformation
to pure spirit might be dismissed as "the delusion of mistaken opinion" but remarks that "perhaps" such an event
did occur "for who has returned from that unknown world
to explain by what forms, and in what manner, he has been
introduced into its aweful precincts." As Natty expires,
Cooper confirms the justice of Middleton's impression.
Again, the sun surrounds Natty with its light, "solemn awe"
fills the assembled company, the old man rises to his feet,
looks toward the heavens, and pronounces "the word—
Here!" (477–78).

Virtually every discussion of *The Prairie* has noted
Cooper's inflation of Natty's character. In accounting for
that narrative strategy, the novel's critics have emphasized
Cooper's intention to separate Natty from the figures who
surround him. He becomes, from the perspective of this
analysis, a symbol of lost possibility, a foil for the flawed
society that replaces him.[15] It is certainly true that Cooper
locates Natty on an elevated plane of experience, but his
portrayal of the trapper is not divergent from but consistent with his descriptions of the novel's other characters.
Just as Ishmael Bush, Inez de Certavallos, and Duncan
Middleton are exaggerated versions of figures who appear
in *The Pioneers* and *Mohicans*, the Natty of *The Prairie*
is an expanded avatar of his former selves. His distance
from the Leatherstocking of *The Pioneers* and the Hawk-
eye of *Mohicans* is congruent with the gap that separates
Inez from Major Effingham and Colonel Munro, Duncan
Middleton from Oliver Effingham and Duncan Heyward,

15 See, e.g., Richard Chase, *The American Novel and Its Tradition*,
52–65.

and Ishmael Bush from Jotham Riddel, the restless borderer of *The Pioneers*. Moreover, Natty's dramatic appearance in the novel parallels Cooper's introductions of his
other characters. Ishmael immediately destroys the single
stand of cottonwood within eyesight; Inez appears from
her tent as a "silent wonder" who excites awe and astonishment; Middleton introduces himself as the grandson of
Heyward and the namesake of Uncas. Cooper defines not
only Natty but all of his characters as archetypes. None of
these figures develop in the course of the novel, nor are
they properly characters. They are rather, from their first
appearances in the novel, fully realized emblems of American possibility.

Cooper's abstract approach to characterization in *The
Prairie* is also evident in his subsidiary figures. Obed Bat
is a caricature of the rationalist. His name, like Ishmael's
and Duncan Uncas Middleton's, is an index to his perspective. Blinded by hubris, he extends the ideals of
the Enlightenment to a ludicrous extreme. He attempts
to impose absolute order on nature through scientific classi-
fication, an effort which miscarries when he mistakes his
own ass for a new genus which he names, in honor of himself, *Verspetilio Horribilis Americanus*. Bat regrets nature's failings and argues that were he entrusted with its
design he could improve the quadruped species by sub-
stituting wheels or levers for "two of the inferior limbs."
Though such an alteration is, he admits, "hopeless—at
least for the present," he anticipates that the expansion of
human reason will someday bring such glory within his
grasp by making man "the master of all learning, and con-
sequently equal to the great moving principle" (224).
The butt of Cooper's clumsy humor, Bat is not just a stock

comic character drawn on the lines of Dickon Jones in *The Pioneers* or David Gamut in *Mohicans*, but another link in Cooper's great chain of national being.

Paul Hover is portrayed in similarly prototypic terms. As a bee hunter and gatherer of honey, he is a figure who explicitly suggests the initial gains of settlement. Bees had long been associated in America with the westward progress of the nation. In accounts ranging from Edwin James's narrative of Stephen Long's 1819 expedition on the Great Plains—Cooper's primary source for *The Prairie*—to Washington Irving's *A Tour on the Prairies* (1835), bees are described as the heralds of settlement, harbingers who announce the explorer's return to civilization.[16] By virtue of his occupation, Hover typifies the stage of social development which followed on the heels of the squatter. More disciplined and stable than Ishmael Bush, and yet still erratic and suspicious of the law, he stands between the primitive order of the Bush family and the refinement of Duncan Middleton.

The Pawnee and Sioux tribesmen of the novel, and more particularly their chieftains, Hard-Heart and Mahtoree, are idealized versions of good and bad Indians. They too are iconic rather than individualized figures, but they differ in one extent from the rest of Cooper's cast. Rather than expanding the scales of analogous characters from the first two Tales, they duplicate the features of Cooper's other Indians. Mahtoree reenacts the role of Magua; Hard-Heart is identified as a Pawnee version of Uncas. The constancy of Cooper's Indians does not, however,

16 See Orm Överland, *The Prairie: The Making and Meaning of an American Classic* (New York, 1967), 48. See, too, *The Oak Openings* (1848), another novel in which Cooper's yeoman hero is a gatherer of honey.

represent a departure from his narrative strategy in *The Prairie*, but suggests instead his ethnocentrism. Like the majority of his contemporaries, Cooper was incapable of conceptualizing Indians in anything other than stereotypic terms. Either as romantic figures who evoked a melancholy meditation on the mutability of time or as personifications of evil and human depravity, his Mohicans and Hurons, his Pawnees and Sioux, are consistently realized as beings larger than life.[17]

Cooper's purpose in abstracting the characters of *The Prairie* parallels his intention in pressing the novel's historical frame to the absolute beginning and end of American development. On one level, his emblematic characters advance Cooper's desire to portray the full range of national experience. By assembling representatives of every level of social evolution in a single novel, he offers a comprehensive survey of American life.[18] In so doing, he strengthens his claim for national particularity. As Henry Nash Smith has suggested, Americans of Cooper's generation argued that while other nations had experienced the same process of cultural development which *The Prairie* describes, only in America were types of each phase of that process simultaneously present.[19]

More important, Cooper's characters forward his efforts to define the shape of American history in a schematic fashion. In *The Prairie* Cooper does not advance his historio-

17 That failure is an understandable one. Cooper met only isolated survivors of dispossessed tribes and noble delegates of the western nations who had traveled to Washington to negotiate treaties. For a comprehensive survey of Cooper's knowledge of the American Indian, see James Franklin Beard's introduction to the SUNY edition of *Mohicans*.

18 The range of Cooper's characterization in *The Prairie* is a further indication of his interest in the epic during this period of his career.

19 Smith, 254–55.

graphic perspective by crafting particular examples which illustrate general principles of development. Ishmael Bush and Inez de Certavallos are not simply metaphors for two forms of social organization; they are the literal embodiment of radical originality and submissive derivation. Their confrontation in the novel is a form of symbolic logic; its resolution carries the force of a theorem rather than an illustration. Cooper has reversed the strategies of the first two Tales. Rather than offering examples to support his overarching vision of American history, he frames an abstraction which may then be applied to particular periods of national life.

But in shifting the plane of his discourse, Cooper has not altered his conception of the determining pattern of American development. Again he forges a potentially destructive conflict between two conceptions of cultural possibility. Ishmael Bush and his family speak for the repudiation of historical entailment. Their opposition to property rights, to law, and to secular and religious institutions of any kind identifies them as proponents of a ceaseless process of new beginnings. In refusing to acknowledge the right of any man to "portion nature out into parcels," they extend to an absurd length Jefferson's axiom that "the earth belongs in usufruct to the living."[20] Jefferson's insistence that every contract, like every constitution, should expire after nineteen years represented a theoretical commitment to the free circulation of property and the primacy of the present, but the Bush family's assault on entailment is literal. Grotesque images of an originality gone mad, Ishmael and his family transform Jefferson's dream of a physio-

20 *The Papers of Thomas Jefferson*, ed. Julian P. Boyd, et al. (Princeton, 1950–74), 15:392.

cratic Eden committed to constant renewal into a nightmare replete with murdered sheriffs, kidnapped brides, and locustlike predators.

Inez de Certvallos defends the historical determinism the Bush family repudiates. Subservient to cultural and religious traditions, she demands imitation from Middleton as the price of her favor. In acceding to her wish that he become like her father "in *every* thing," Middleton would sacrifice freedom for enslavement, free choice for dependence. Inez's small frame and her impotence in the face of captors—as well as her Spanish heritage—suggest for Cooper not the highest achievement of civilization, as Orm Överland has argued, but the decadence and cultural eclipse which must follow the surrender of American authority to oligarchic interests.[21]

But despite their diametric opposition, both Inez and the Bush family are bound by the limits of a partriarchal system. Inez conforms to the wishes of both Don Augustin, her natural father, and Father Ignatius, her spiritual guide. Her decisions are determined by their judgments; her character has been shaped by their perspectives. She does not declare her freedom from their authority by marrying Middleton but becomes, instead, a missionary for their cause. The primitive form of government that unifies the Bush family is also predicated upon a submission of individual will to paternal power. Having rejected civil and religious sanctions, Bush adopts brute force to impose familial discipline. He cows his sons with his strength and demands absolute obedience to his commands. The most frightening of Cooper's many father figures, he crushes the initiative of his sons to ensure that "disorder don't spread" (110).

21 Överland, 158.

When Asa, Ishmael's firstborn, is mysteriously murdered
shortly after he has contested Bush's leadership, the two
events acquire a causal connection. Although Ishmael is
innocent of that crime and ultimately avenges his son's
murder, Asa's death, as William Wasserstrom has observed, is closely linked with his rebellion against his
father.[22]

The Prairie's logic is unmistakable. Both Bush's repudiation of historical context and Inez's enslavement to
it result in tyranny. Neither the anarchic originality of the
squatter nor the passive submission of the heiress are capable of promoting progress or security. Cooper's alternative is the moderate course of Duncan Middleton. By
liberating Inez from both Bush's camp and her father's
home, Middleton preserves the integrity of social order,
while he undermines its repressive force. An opponent of
the novel's father figures and a defender of the tradition
initiated by his grandfather, Middleton—and by extension the culture he serves—are both free from, and bound
to, history. As he does in *The Pioneers* and *Mohicans*, Cooper validates Middleton's cultural paternity by describing
his subsequent career. After his return to New Orleans,
Middleton "attracted the attention of the government"
and "was soon employed in various situations of responsibility and confidence" which ultimately lead to a con-
gressional seat. Paul Hover has enjoyed an analogous prosperity. Under Middleton's patronage, his character has
undergone "a great and beneficial change" which Cooper
generalizes as the characteristic progress of his class. Hover,
he writes,

22 Wasserstrom, 423–37.

soon became a landholder, then a prosperous cultivator of the soil, and shortly after a town-officer. By that progressive change in fortunes, which in the republic is so singularly accompanied by a corresponding improvement in knowledge and self-respect, he went on, from step to step, until his wife enjoyed the maternal delight of seeing her children placed far beyond the danger of returning to that state from which both their parents had issued. [466]

The historiographic assumptions Cooper derives from his schematic investigation of American civilization are resolutely meliorist. Telescoping the course of cultural evolution, he offers his readers a model of national development. That growth begins with the violent repudiation of the past, a phase of cultural life Cooper personifies in the Bush family. Their murder of a deputy sheriff and their contempt for institutional restraints document their rejection of the historical process which has yielded civil order. Although their militant originality results in anarchy, they are nonetheless the progenitors of American independence. The Bush family's abduction of Inez is a lamentable act of brigandry, but it is also a blow against European inscription. By kidnapping a character Cooper has identied as both a cultural and a religious icon, they deny the authority of the Old World.

The second stage of American evolution, which Paul Hover and Ellen Wade suggest, redresses the savagery of the squatters by combining a commitment to personal freedom with a rudimentary respect for law and tradition. Hover synthesizes the social orders of the Bush family and Spanish Catholicism and advances the cause of social growth, but his sensibility lacks stability and refinement. It remains for Duncan Middleton to complete the dialectical process which the yeoman class begins. Middleton's role as a mediator is broadly defined: his marriage reconciles European and American culture; his opposition to both Ishmael Bush and Father Ignatius balances anarchy and despotism; his decision to take up residence in New Orleans secures the expansion of American culture and the preservation of a western boundary. Middleton's relationship with Duncan Heyward—and ultimately with Colonel Munro—establishes America's links to the European past, while his figurative kinship with Natty Bumppo reaffirms the nation's independence from that tradition.

From one perspective, then, *The Prairie* is a remarkably coherent novel. By assembling representatives of every phase of American life and by bringing their world views into conflict, Cooper is able to trace the development of American history in a highly focused manner. Moreover, his historical perspective is not subject to the revisions of the future because the Great Plains have effectively blocked western expansion and rendered the authority of Duncan Middleton's class immune to challenge. America's past has been ordered and its future made secure. With a resounding sense of closure, Cooper brings the Leatherstocking series to completion.

But like the conclusions of *The Pioneers* and *Mohicans*, Cooper's confident resolution of *The Prairie*'s tensions is subverted by a series of contradictions. In the first two volumes of the Tales, the rivalry between text and subtext—between Cooper's final assertions and the lingering anxieties they unsuccessfully repress—is only apparent when Cooper generalizes his narrative action. But because *The Prairie* is fundamentally metahistorical in character, its inconsistencies are far more readily apparent. Cooper in this novel does not move from the concrete to the universal but raises the stakes of his fiction. If he can successfully resolve the conflicts of his prototypic characters, he has, by definition, established the shape and direction of American culture. He would then no longer need to argue for the representative nature of his fictional events. But his contention that Middleton has bridged the novel's polarities is extremely troublesome. Nothing in Cooper's narrative suggests that Middleton is capable either of restraining the barbarity of the Bush family or of tempering the repressive culture of the Old World.

By inflating the characters of Ishmael and his family to nightmarish proportions, Cooper has rendered them inaccessible to Middleton's control. In the novel's penultimate scene Ishmael determines the fate of Middleton, Hover, and Natty who stand bound before him. Announcing that "I am called upon this day to fill the office which in the settlements you give unto judges," he enlists the biblical rubric that "an eye must be returned for an eye and a tooth for a tooth" as the determining principle of his court and pledges to "give unto all and each that which is his due and no more." He returns Inez to Middleton because "it was a mistake to take a child from its parent" (426); permits Hover to claim Ellen because he is unwilling to be "a ruler of inclination"; and, after he discovers that Abiram White and not Natty has murdered his son Asa, releases the trapper and condemns his brother-in-law to death (433). In his discussion of *The Prairie*, John P. McWilliams notes the equity of Ishmael's decisions and argues that he "achieves what few of Cooper's frontiersmen ever even attempt. He openly delivers impartial justice according to a fixed and stated principle of moral law." Although that

principle is, McWilliams continues, "based upon a preciv-
ilized conception of justice," Bush's court "brings to the
wilderness Cooper's cornerstone of social order, the civil
law."[23]

This reading of Ishmael's judicial performance as an
indication of regeneration in the lawless squatter, who, in
McWilliams's terms, has gained in stature and has recognized the need for law, is consistent with Cooper's meliorist
vision. It is, however, disjunctive with the spirit of this
text. Cooper certainly intended Ishmael's tribunal to suggest a preliminary version of Judge Temple's courtroom,
but Ishmael remains a frightening emblem of unrestrained
and arbitrary power. That his decisions are ultimately just
does not alter the fact that his authority is self-determined
—that he has "called" himself to "fill the office" of judge.
Rather than as a prisoner before the bar of justice, he defines
and administers the law. Ishmael is not, as McWilliams has
suggested, chastened by his experience or "repulsed by the
harshness of the prairie" but is thoroughly in control of his
destiny and of those of the novel's other characters.[24] "His
self-constituted tribunal," Cooper writes, "excited a degree
of awe to which even the intelligent Middleton could not
bring himself to be entirely insensible" (425). Ishmael
releases Inez and Ellen, not because Middleton has forced
his hand or because "the fear of the law [had] come over"
him, but because he chooses to do so (427). He is not held
accountable for his crimes; Cooper is able to argue only that
"some of the numerous descendents of [Ishmael and Es-
ther] were reclaimed from their lawless and semi-barbaric

23 McWilliams, 269.
24 Ibid., 274.

lives." Ishmael himself returns to the settlements and is "never heard of more" (452).

Middleton's dealings with Don Augustin and Father Ignatius are brought to a similarly unsatisfactory conclusion. Seeking to turn Inez's abduction "to some account in the impending warfare of the faith," Father Ignatius tells his congregation that because of her unfortunate alliance with a heretic she has "been translated to heaven" (202). Her return to New Orleans and Middleton's account of her kidnapping and rescue dispel that claim and embarrass Ignatius. His credibility is undermined among all but the most superstitious of his flock, who preserve their belief "with that species of sublimated and solitary gratification that a miser finds in gazing at his growing, but useless hoard" (465). On the strength of this rather fragile blow against the monolith of Spanish Catholicism, Cooper announces the collapse of opposition to Middleton's religion and political principles. No longer will he be called upon to imitate the Don. But because Cooper depends upon Ignatius's humiliation not only to suggest a cultural repudiation of Old World example but also to defuse the oligarchic potential of American democracy, Middleton's mastery of the priest is grossly overburdened. Cooper again predicates his historical perspective on a resolution which is both contrived and disproportionate to its thematic function.

Two narrative trajectories, then, complicate our reading of *The Prairie*. On one hand, Cooper begins the novel by advancing a thesis. The Louisiana Purchase, he argues, confronted the nation with a serious crisis. The addition of so large a body of territory suggested the prospect of chaos and division. National security was threatened both by the anarchic squatters who "plunged" into the new territories and by the Old World reactionaries who occupied its eastern ranges. But Cooper maintains, through a process of mediation this threat was disarmed and "the wisdom of that measure," i.e., the Louisiana Purchase, "was generally conceded" (9). He then demonstrates the truth of his proposition. The Bush family is returned to the control of law, Spanish culture is peacefully subsumed, and a western boundary is established. In the novel's conclusion, Cooper restates his meliorist thesis and, by describing the successful careers of Middleton and Hover, affirms the dialectical character of American history.

The narrative events Cooper employs as evidence to support his historiographic assumptions are, however, inadequate to their purpose and generate a divergent reading of America's past and future. The moderate principles Middleton defends are clearly impotent in the face of Bush's barbarity and suspiciously vulnerable to the entrenched Catholicism of New Orleans. *The Prairie*'s development does not strengthen Cooper's assurances of the ultimate triumph of Middleton's class, but suggests instead a conception of American history as a collision between irreconcilable polarities. The anarchy of the Bush family seems to demand the repressive force of totalitarianism. Autocratic rule, in turn, seems invulnerable to any remedy other than the radicalism of the squatters. Cooper's doubled vision of American history as a simultaneous realization of originality and tradition becomes a fantasy inconsistent with the divergent potentials of democracy.

Rather than resolving the difficulties of *The Pioneers* and *Mohicans*, Cooper's metahistorical posture has exacerbated them. Bush and Inez extend the potency of analogous characters in the first two Tales, but even as a prototypic mediator, Middleton occupies essentially the same position as Oliver Effingham and Duncan Heyward. As such, he is confronted by a more difficult task than either Effingham or Heyward and is ultimately dwarfed by characters whose power he must temper. As a result, *The Prairie* is not a work of certain definition but a manifestation of a fundamental cultural dilemma. Its theoretical demonstration of American progress defines the nation's aspirations, while its unresolved tensions confirm its fears. A novel which begins as an attempt to contain American experience becomes a self-deconstructing work in which Cooper's historiographic intentions are frustrated by his inability to enact them.

Two of *The Prairie*'s subsidiary themes reproduce the confusion implicit in Cooper's historical perspective. The diametric opposition Cooper establishes between Ishmael and Inez is paralleled by the equally polar conflict of Natty and Obed Bat. Bat's belief in human perfectibility prompts him to argue that although the history of civilization "teaches the natural depravity of the *genus* . . . if science could be fairly brought to bear on a whole species at once —education might eradicate the evil principle." Natty vigorously rejects Bat's hubristic conception of American possibility. "That for your education!" he tells the naturalist,

> The time has been when I have thought it possible to make a companion of a beast. Many are the cubs, and many are the speckled fawns that I have reared with these old hands, until I have even fancied them rational and altered beings—but what did it amount to? the bear would bite, and the deer would run, notwithstanding my wicked conceit in fancying I

could change a temper that the Lord himself had seen fit to bestow. Now if man is so blinded in his folly as to go on, ages on ages, doing harm chiefly to himself, there is the same reason to think that he has wrought evil here as in the countries you call so old. [297]

Natty defends this deterministic view of human history by arguing that the emptiness of the Great Plains is itself a testament to human folly. Maintaining that a great civilization had once occupied the prairie, he asks Bat "where are the multitudes that once peopled these prairies; the kings and palaces; the richness and mightiness of this desert."[25] When Bat demands that Natty locate the monuments which might "prove the truth of so vague a theory," Natty tells him that the erosions of time have displaced them even more thoroughly than the ruins of ancient Egypt and Rome.

> They are gone. Time has lasted too long for them. For why? Time was made by the Lord, and they were made by men. This very spot of reeds and grass, on which you now sit, may once have been the garden of some mighty king. It is the fate of all things to ripen, and then decay. The tree blossoms, and bears its fruit, which falls, rots, withers, and even the seed is lost! Go, count the rings of the oak and of the sycamore; they lie in circles, one about another, until the eye is blinded in striving to make out their numbers; and yet a full change of the seasons comes round while the stem is winding one of these little lines about itself, like the buffalo changing his coat, or the buck his horns; and what does it all amount to? [298]

Bat's dispute with Natty renews one of the central issues of *Mohicans*. In that novel, Cooper repressed the anxieties attendant to the potential decline of American

25 See Ringe's discussion of this passage in *Pictorial Mode*, 131–33.

culture by arguing that the nation might avoid the fate of Europe and the tribes by preserving its independence from their corruption. By establishing a lineage that extends from Natty to Duncan Heyward and finally to the American people at large, he argues for an "exceptional" status which would deflect, or at least postpone, national decline. That strategy is, as I have argued, flawed by a contradiction between Cooper's sense of human constancy and his conception of American difference. In *The Prairie* that disjunction of logic is even more pronounced. Natty, whose repudiation of civilized and savage depravity serves as the source of America's separation from the spiral of historical decline, is, in this novel, both remote from the culture that will embody his principles and thoroughly convinced of the impossibility of human renewal.

Cooper continues to describe Middleton, and the nation whose progress he promotes, as the heirs of Natty's values, but his narrative strongly suggests that Natty's world view is inaccessible to *The Prairie*'s other characters. By expanding Natty's character to a superhuman proportion, Cooper has removed him from his role as a cultural initiator. He has become a detached commentator on human folly, a resigned spectator who sadly observes the constant repetition of weakness and error. In that capacity, Natty advances a perspective which acquires the power of incontrovertible truth. Although Cooper tempers Natty's pronouncements about the inevitability of corruption and decline by describing his argument with Bat as "erratic discourse," he is incapable of reversing the authority he has ceded to Natty. His rebuttal of Bat's boundless meliorism possesses an integrity which Cooper's optimistic conclusion cannot subvert. Regardless of his assurance that the twin threats of anarchy and authoritarianism have been defused, Natty's skepticism about the nation's future undermines the optimism of *The Prairie*'s resolution.

The enduring force of Natty's cyclical conception of history presents a particularly severe problem for Cooper because that vision denies any possibility of American difference. Natty angrily rejects Bat's celebration of the "treasures and glories" of Europe. "*Old* World!" he exclaims

> that is the miserable cry of all the half-starved miscreants that have come into this blessed land since the days of my boyhood! They tell you of the *Old* World; as if the Lord had not the power and the will to create the universe in a day, or as if he had not bestowed his gifts with an equal hand, though not with an equal mind, or equal wisdom, have they been received and used. Were they to say a *worn* out, and an *abused* and a *sacrilegious* world, they might not be so far from truth! [249]

But despite this chauvinistic posture, Natty also maintains that in all places "mankind twist and turn the rules of the Lord to suit their own wickedness," and that man "has wrought his evil here as in the countries you call so old" (297). The divergence between Natty's rejection of the Old World and his insistence on human constancy parallels Cooper's own dilemma in *The Prairie*. The dialectical character of his conclusion announces America's departure from Old World precedent; his meliorist perspective denies the circularity of time. But Cooper's failure to demonstrate persuasively Middleton's triumph compromises the credibility of these positions. Like Natty, Cooper declaims against Old World corruption, but his narrative supports a static conception of human possibility. The fathers Cooper attempts to displace in *The Prairie*—Ishmael Bush, Don Augustin, and Father Ignatius—are not fully vanquished.

They conveniently resign their authority to Middleton, but they are by no means overthrown. The prospect of an American dominated either by the originality of Ishmael Bush or by the dependence of Inez de Certavallos retains its power.

A second contradiction involves Cooper's treatment of his Indian characters. Like Jefferson and Madison, who during their presidential tenures advocated the removal of the eastern tribes to the Louisiana territories, and like his contemporaries who defended that removal as a means of protecting the endangered tribes and of opening new lands for settlement and exploitation, Cooper hoped that the tribes might be peacefully relocated in the Great Plains. That resettlement would, he believed, resolve the nagging question of Indian rights and bring an end to two centuries of national dishonor.[26] In *The Prairie*, he imaginatively realizes that desire by returning his white characters to the Mississippi's eastern bank. The Pawnee and the Sioux retain the possession of their hunting grounds; the troubling dispossessions of *The Pioneers* and *Mohicans* are avoided. Cooper's efforts to bring a sense of closure to the nation's history encompasses, then, even the loose ends of the Indian Wars. The long history of tribal betrayal is resolved, and a new era of race relations is launched. Hard-Heart, the Uncas figure of *The Prairie*, becomes the figurative son of Natty and brother of Duncan Middleton. The cultural harmony unavailable to Cooper in *Mohicans* is achieved in what Cooper assumed would be the saga's final volume.

But like Middleton's ascendancy over Ishmael Bush and Father Ignatius, Cooper's projection of racial harmony conflicts with *The Prairie*'s trajectory. By describing Hard-

26 See Cooper's discussion of Indian resettlement in *Notions* 1:277–88.

Heart's confrontation with Mahtoree as an almost identical reenactment of Uncas's struggle with Magua, Cooper
implies—as Donald Ringe has argued—that "the process
that began on the eastern seaboard with the dislocation of
the Delawares and the settling of the forest wilderness now
moves into its final stage."[27] When Hard-Heart rejects
Mahtoree's argument that the tribes should resolve their
enmities to unite against the white invaders, and then in
single combat kills and scalps him, the ironies of *Mohicans*
are repeated with renewed intensity. The price of being a
good Indian is, in Cooper's terms, a compromising alliance
with white characters who will ultimately displace all of the
tribes. Cooper attempts to resolve that paradox by permitting Hard-Heart to survive the novel's conflicts, but as
the Indian chieftain stands beside the dying Natty in the
novel's final chapter, his fate, despite Cooper's assurances
that American expansion will end at the prairies, seems in-
exorably aligned with that of the trapper. Just as Natty
has been the agent of his own dispossession, the virtuous
Hard-Heart has sealed his doom by refusing Mahtoree's
proffered alliance. One need not cite the Trail of Tears, the
massacre at Tippecanoe, or the expansion of John Jacob
Astor's trading empire in the Rockies to discredit Cooper's
conception of an Indian homeland as an illusion. The
lengthy shadow of the Bush family and the echoes of
Mohicans are sufficient for that purpose. Cooper's final
image of Hard-Heart's isolation on the plains is as wistful
as his account of Bush's return to the Mississippi. Strained
desires, they remain inconsistent with *The Prairie*'s narrative force.

In arguing that the historiographic confusion of *The*

27 Donald A. Ringe, *James Fenimore Cooper* (New Haven, 1962), 46.

Pioneers and *The Last of the Mohicans* becomes explicit in *The Prairie*, I am, of course, describing that novel as a pivotal work in Cooper's canon. Although the optimistic conclusion of this volume of the Tales, demonstrates Cooper's unwillingness to abandon the doubled historical perspective of *The Pioneers* and *Mohicans*, that paradigm has lost its power. Middleton's reconciliation of the novel's polarities is entirely unpersuasive, and as a result, Cooper's doubled vision of America as a culture free from, and bound to, the past is incapable of compelling our belief. In its place, we are left with a sense of national history as a battleground on which the forces of originality and dependence will ceaselessly collide.

Accounting for this breakdown in Cooper's narrative strategy is more difficult than describing it. Biographical evidence suggests that at the time of *The Prairie*'s publication, Cooper was as content with his lot as he was ever to be. He was comfortably settled in Falbourg St. Germain where he enjoyed the respect of the French social and literary establishments, and although his finances were still precarious, the success of *Mohicans* both at home and abroad had eased his concerns.[28] Prior to his departure from America in 1826, he had been lionized by his New York friends at a farewell banquet and had been warmly received in the Washington office of Secretary of State Henry Clay.[29] His preeminence as America's leading novelist was secure; he could now list General Lafayette and Sir Walter Scott among his friends and admirers. Indeed, the unrestrained nationalism of *Notions of the Americans* (1828), the fictional travelogue Cooper published immediately after *The*

28 *L&J* 1:127; Överland, p. 19.
29 *L&J* 1:139–41; *L&J* 1:136, 137n.

Prairie, seems more consistent with his state of mind than the troubling text of that work.

When we turn, however, from the tranquil circumstances of Cooper's life to consider the implications of his choice of setting in *The Prairie*, the novel's foreboding quality becomes somewhat more understandable. By locating *The Prairie* in the Great Plains rather than in the forests of New York, Cooper sacrificed the ready evidence of social progress available to him in *The Pioneers* and *Mohicans*. Not only did the still unsettled environs of the prairies lack the reassuring presence of "beautiful and thriving villages," but they also introduced a problematic context. From the first days of the Louisiana Purchase, the trans-Mississippi west had provoked broadly shared anxieties. Although the nation's initial response to the acquisition of the Louisiana territories had been primarily positive, many Americans saw the New West as a source of division and decline. Disgruntled New England Federalists, who attacked the Purchase as a threat to national security, worried that unlimited settlement would foster anarchy and chaos.[30] Fisher Ames, one of the most strident members of the Federalist camp, insisted, for example, that America had now become "too big for union, too sordid for patriotism, too democratic for liberty." The Louisiana Purchase, he concluded, would send the nation "rushing like a comet into infinite space." Senator Thomas Pickering of Massachusetts took Ames's objections one step further and argued that "The principles

---

30 New England opposition to the Purchase crystallized when Federalist leaders in Massachusetts and Connecticut secretly proposed the formation of an independent Northern Confederacy. Arguing that the addition of the Louisiana territories had upset the balance of power on which the Constitution was predicated, they called for the secession of New England and New York from the newly expanded union.

of our Revolution point to the remedy—a separation."[31] In Virginia, a number of Jefferson's fellow republicans shared the misgivings of Ames and Pickering and condemned the Purchase as a violation of states' rights. By increasing dramatically the nation's size and by promising citizenship to an alien people, Jefferson had, they maintained, assumed an authority not explicitly granted in the Constitution and had undermined the foundations of American government.[32]

These initial objections to the acquisition of Louisiana were largely theoretical, but as territorial immigration both east and west of the Mississippi increased in the decade between 1810 and 1820, the frontier became the locus of more practical concern. The political imperatives of the region— its commitment to expanded suffrage, internal improvements, and easy credit—greatly exacerbated the North-South cleavage which had shaped national politics since the Revolution. Compromise became more difficult; the business of government more complex. Eastern legislators came to regard themselves as the defenders of national tradition and resisted with mounting vigor the diminution of their power. The corrosive debate over the War of 1812 focused the resultant threat to American union with frightening clarity. Spurred by their desires to annex Canada and to crush the western tribes, territorial delegates aligned with their southern colleagues to press for war with Great Britain. New England, whose industrial and shipping interests would presumably suffer in such a conflict, opposed—almost

31 Quoted in Samuel Eliot Morison, *The Oxford History of the American People* (New York, 1965), 368.
32 Like New England's scruples, Virginia's objections to the Purchase diminished as the material advantages of American sovereignity in Louisiana became increasingly more apparent.

to the point of treason—the demands of the war hawks. The region's representatives, embittered by the pro-French sympathies of the Madison administration and frightened by their growing impotence, tentatively introduced the prospect of secession. At the height of the war, Massachusetts convened a New England convention at Hartford to confer upon "their public grievances and concerns . . . and also to take measures, if they shall think proper, for procuring a conventions of delegates from all the United States, in order to revise the Constitution thereof."[33] Secessionists' attempts to sever the thirteen original states from the western territories miscarried, but the disruptive potential of new sectional alliances was clearly established.

During the Era of Good Feelings which followed the war, regional rivalry abated to some degree, but an illusive quest for a lasting synthesis continued to dominate the nation's agenda. In the legislative measures introduced by Henry Clay, Daniel Webster, and John C. Calhoun, in the rhetoric of Fourth of July orations, and in the slogans of road builders and manufacturers, the same conjunction of aspiration and anxiety recurs. Americans universally defended the cause of national union but remained skeptical about its prospects. Thomas Jefferson, for example, spoke of the sacred character of the union but wrote from retirement that the Missouri Compromise of 1820 had "like a fire bell in the night, awakened and filled me with terror. . . . I considered it at once as the death knell of the union." John Quincy Adams, whose presidential tenure would be devoted to balancing sectional interests, agreed with Jefferson's gloomy appraisal. "I take it for granted," he argued,

33 See Theodore Dwight, *History of the Hartford Convention* (New York, 1906), 11.

"that the present question is mere preamble . . . a title page to a great tragic volume."[34] The partisan spirit of the elections of 1824 and 1828 confirmed the legitimacy of those fears, but the coming of Jacksonian democracy only dramatized the regional and class differences which had by then become unmistakable.

By setting *The Prairie* in the New West, Cooper necessarily predicated the novel's dialectical structure on faith rather than extrapolation. At a time in which the specter of national disruption loomed very large indeed, Cooper reaffirms his vision of American history and assures his readers of the constancy of national tradition. But like Jefferson, Cooper too heard a firebell in the night. He tells us in *The Prairie*'s concluding sentence that Natty's tombstone reads, "May no wanton hand ever disturb his remains!" Cooper's "may" speaks less as a command than as a longing. As much an exercise in wish-fulfillment as his announcement of the closing of the frontier, Natty's epitaph is an injunction whose very wording questions its authority.

The correspondence between Cooper's synthesis of doubt and desire and the structure of feeling present in his cultural context should not obscure, however, the determining role of *The Prairie*'s status as the third volume of a fictional series. It is a testament to Cooper's ambition that he does not simply renew the syntax of the earlier Tales but attempts instead to expand their resonance. The weight of self-consciousness is, however, too great a burden for Cooper's doubled vision to bear. Regardless of the contradictory character of *The Pioneers* and *Mohicans*, Cooper's resolution of their narrative tensions is plausible within their textual worlds. Such is not the case in *The Prairie*. Here, Coo-

34 Quoted in Morison, 405.

per commits himself to self-analysis and demonstrates not the certain truth of his historical perspective but, rather, its irredeemable flaws.

Independent of any external considerations, *The Prairie* is a work which overturns Cooper's prior logic. In the manner of a scientist who submits a previously viable hypothesis to a more rigid examination, Cooper tests the assumptions of *The Pioneers* and *Mohicans* and undermines their power as accounting strategies. An acknowledgment of that loss is not the province of *The Prairie* but of the last two volumes of the Tales. To some degree, as I shall argue, the unmediated polarities of those novels follow from Cooper's disillusionment with the course of American democracy, but his perspective in these works is less the result of his disaffection than it is the product of his failure to sustain the wistful duality of *The Pioneers* and *The Last of the Mohicans*.

∞ 4 ∞
The Pathfinder
and the Limits
of Originality
∞※∞

If thou beest hee; But O how fall'n! how chang'd
From him, who in the happy Realms of Light
Cloth'd with transcendent brightness didst outshine
Myriads though bright . . .

—Paradise Lost

THIRTEEN years after the publication of *The Prairie*,
Cooper returned to the Leatherstocking Tales by reinvoking
the *donnée* and the narrative progress of *The Last of the
Mohicans*. Like *Mohicans*, *The Pathfinder* (1840) begins
with the journey of a young woman to a frontier outpost
where her father serves with the British army. Again that
passage is imperiled by a treacherous Indian guide, whose
malevolent intentions are frustrated by the timely intervention of Natty and Chingachgook. Natty is as quick to
detect Arrowhead's villainy as he was to identify Magua as
a traitor. He supplants him as the party's leader, repels an
Iroquois ambush, and successfully conveys Mabel Dunham
to the British garrison at Lake Ontario. Mabel's reunion
with Sergeant Dunham is, however, as brief as that of the
Munro sisters with their father. In a scene reminiscent of
the William Henry massacre, the Sergeant's expeditionary
force is attacked and brutally slaughtered. Mabel is cap-

tured by Arrowhead and threatened, as Cora Munro was, with the prospect of an Indian marriage. Of course, Natty rescues her from captivity and returns Mabel to Ontario. There she marries Jasper Western, the captain of a Great Lakes' cutter, and together they bid farewell to Natty and Chingachgook, who retreat once more to the forest.[1]

As in *Mohicans*, Cooper employs the French and Indian Wars to frame two equally futile possibilities for national development. Again, both an unquestioning adherence to convention and unprincipled departure from traditional values result in chaos and death. Sergeant Dunham and his superior officers repeat the mistakes of Munro, Webb, and Braddock by refusing to observe the precautions their frontier circumstances require. They cling repeatedly to the military codes of Europe and squander the opportunities of the New World. Tribal leadership is similarly recalcitrant. Cooper's warriors fail to overcome their rivalries and ensure their annihilation by aligning themselves with the British and French. An amoral negation of convention is, however, no more conducive to personal or cultural security than it was in *Mohicans*. Both Arrowhead and Lieutenant Muir, the garrison's quartermaster, subordinate loyalty to greed, and pay for their treachery with their lives. Captain Sanglier, the French liason to the Iroquois, adopts the practices of the tribes and organizes an effective fighting force, but because he abandons Christian sanctions along with the codes of European warfare, he becomes, like Montcalm, a moral bankrupt.

The assumptions Cooper derives from this record of

---

1 Cooper's use of the narrative structure of *Mohicans* is certainly a conscious one. Throughout *The Pathfinder*, Natty recalls his adventures with the Munro sisters and compares Mabel's journey to Ontario with their passage to William Henry.

European and Indian error are consistent with those of
Mohicans. He considers the conflicting claims of originality
and dependence and defines each of those unmediated cultural trajectories as destructive for American interests. The
French and Indian Wars again suggest the fatal implications
of a slavish conventionality. Just as they refuse American
venison and salmon for Scottish oat cakes, the British soldiers at Ontario reject colonial advice and preserve the
military protocol of Europe. When, for example, Mabel
warns Corporal McNab of an impending ambush, he dismisses her fears and insists that "this American mode of
fighting that is getting into so much favor, will destroy the
reputation of His Majesty's army, if it no destroy its
spirit." Take "the word of an old soldier, who has seen
his fifty-fifth year," he tells her, "there is no surer method
to encourage your enemy, than to seem to fear him; and
that there is no danger in this Indian warfare, that the fan-
cies and imaginations of your Americans have not augmented and enlarged upon until they see a savage in every
bush. We Scots come from a naked region, and have no
need, and less relish for covers."[2] Rather than alerting his
troops, he lectures Mabel on Scottish military history, a lesson that is interrupted by an Indian bullet which claims
McNab's life. Cooper generalizes McNab's arrogance by
describing him as "an epitome, though on a scale suited
to his rank, of those very qualities, which were so peculiar
to the servants of the crown, that were sent into the colonies,
as these servants estimated themselves in comparison with
the natives of the country, or, in other words, he considered

2 James Fenimore Cooper, *The Pathfinder* (Albany, N. Y., 1981),
p. 338. Future references will be to this edition and will be cited by page
number in the text.

the American as an animal inferior to the parent stock, and
viewed all his notions of military service in particular as
undigested and absurd" (335).

McNab's commanding officer, Major Duncan, is also
the victim of a culturally induced blindness. He criticizes
Dunham's reliance on Natty and Chingachgook to provide
his men with venison as a mistake characteristic of his
"American birth, and American training." A "thorough soldier," he tells Dunham, never "relies on any thing but his
commissary for supplies, and I beg that no part of my regiment may be the first to set an example to the contrary."
Echoing the opinion of McNab, he maintains that "the ir-
regularity of the provincials has played the devil with the
King's service too often to be winked at any longer" (192).
Duncan's unwillingness to admit the value of colonial judgment is compounded by his unexamined commitment to an
Old World perspective. Not only does he accept without
question British colonial policy, but he suspends as well his
objectivity in dealing with his subordinates. He doubts the
loyalty of Jasper Western because Jasper speaks French,
and distrusts Dunham because of his colonial heritage. He
never questions, however, the honor of the renegade Lieutenant Muir because Muir is both a Scotsman and his boyhood friend.

As lamentable as Cooper finds European and Indian
conventionality, he regards that obstinance as less irrational
than colonial submission to British authority. Cooper describes that dependence as an attribute of a prerevolutionary childhood. "America," he observes,

> at the time of which we are writing, was remarkable for its
> attachment to the German family that then sat on the British
> throne, for, as is the fact with all provinces, the virtues and

qualities that are proclaimed near the centre of power, as in-
cense and policy, get to be a part of political faith, with the
credulous and ignorant at a distance. This truth is just as
apparent today, in connection with the prodigies of the republic,
as it then was in connection with those distant rulers, whose
merits it was always safe to applaud, and whose demerits it was
treason to reveal. It is a consequence of this mental dependence,
that public opinion is so much placed at the mercy of the design-
ing, and the world in the midst of its idle boasts of knowledge
and improvement, is left to receive its truths, on all such points
as touch the interests of the powerful and managing, through
such a medium and such a medium only, as may serve the
particular views of those who pull the wires. Pressed upon by
the subjects of France, who were then encircling the British
colonies, with a belt of forts and settlements that completely
secured the savages for allies, it would have been difficult to
say, whether the Americans loved the English more than they
hated the French, and those who then lived would have considered the alliance which took place between the cis-Atlantic
subjects, and the ancient rivals of the British Crown, some
twenty years later, as an event entirely without the circle of
probabilities. [212]

Sergeant Dunham is Cooper's primary example of this
"mental dependence." Despite his national pride, which
prompts him to remind Major Duncan of Braddock's refusal to accept Washington's advice at Duquesne, and despite the prejudice he has experienced from his British colleagues, Dunham, like Duncan Heyward, has adopted a
European perspective. He accepts Duncan's argument that
Jasper's bilingualism compromises his honor even though
he has served with Jasper and witnessed his bravery.
Seduced by that British suspicion, he relieves Jasper of his
command of *The Scud* and entrusts the ship to his brother-
in-law, Charles Cap. An oceangoing seaman, Cap has had no
experience on Ontario and nearly sinks *The Scud*. Jasper

rescues the ship, but Dunham does not profit from this lesson. Shortly after *The Scud* has been righted, he again subordinates native wit to British convention. He fails to reconnoiter his camp when he returns from an attack on the French and blunders unarmed into an ambush. Although Jasper and Natty redeem Dunham's mission, the Sergeant is mortally wounded and his troops suffer heavy casualties. The parallel Cooper establishes between Dunham and McNab is an obvious one. Both men are victims of a failure of vision. They recognize neither the Iroquois who wait in ambush nor the necessity of abandoning European strategies in the wilderness. McNab's blindness anticipates the decline of Old World authority; Dunham's error suggests the more threatening eclipse of America's promise.

Cooper considers the consequences of dependence not only on a cultural level but on a social, a familial, and an individual plane as well. He dramatizes, for example, the rigidity of Fort Ontario's social hierarchy by describing Mabel's status among the women of the garrison. Her personal merit is more than sufficient to establish her as an equal of the officers' wives, but her father's rank excludes her from a full association with them. When Jasper gives Mabel a calash he has won in a shooting match, the ladies debate "the fitness of so handsome a thing's passing into the possession of a non-commissioned officer's child." A captain's wife tells her that it is "an article of dress you can never wear" and offers to buy it from her. When Mabel modestly refuses to part with Jasper's gift, the woman accuses her of a lack of prudence and tells her to remember that "if you do determine to dispose of the thing . . . it is bespoke, and that I will not take it, if you ever even put it on your own head" (168). Cooper is not assuming a leveling position in this

scene; indeed, he respects in principle the garrison's attention to rank. But he does insist that a society which preserves
historically determined boundaries without providing access
to merit inevitably acts against its interests and promotes
stagnation and decline.

That assertion is further grounded by Cooper's consideration of the paternal discipline Sergeant Dunham attempts to impose on Mabel. Having decided that Natty
will be her husband, Dunham dismisses the scout's misgivings and assures him that "the hussy would never dream
of refusing to marry a man who was her father's friend before she was born" (132). He rejects Major Duncan's suggestion that Mabel be permitted to choose her own husband
by telling him that "disobedience is the next crime to
mutiny" and insists that his daughter must subordinate her
desire to his authority (196). Although he tempers his
rhetoric when he presses Mabel to accept Natty's proposal,
he establishes his preference in a manner that gives his
daughter little choice. "If I could see you promised to Pathfinder—know that you were pledged to be his wife," he says,
"let my own fate be what it might, I think I could die happy.
But I will ask no pledge of you my child—I will not force
you to do what you might repent. Kiss me, Mabel, and go to
your bed" (311). Mabel, Cooper reports, had been "trained
like a woman to subdue her most ardent feeling" and surrenders her will to her father. "God blesses the dutiful
daughter," she tells Dunham, "I will marry whomever you
desire" (312).

Cooper clarifies his disapproval of Dunham's coercive
tactics by implicitly linking his despotism with that of the
corrupt Tuscarora guide Arrowhead, who imposes his will
on his submissive wife, Dew-of-June, with no regard for

her wishes or her safety. He continually rebukes her for hesitating even slightly in the performance of her duties and threatens to kill her if she violates his orders. Cooper's accounts of June's passive obedience and Arrowhead's malignant rage are consistent with his stereotypic conception of Indians, but their relationship significantly glosses Dunham's dealings with his daughter. Like Arrowhead, the Sergeant has overstepped what Cooper regards as the legitimate power of a husband and father to become a tyrant whose authority must be broken by rebellion. In this context, June's passivity is a cautionary tale. When Arrowhead is killed in the novel's concluding episode, she refuses to leave his graveside until Natty forcibly removes her to Mabel's cabin. Unwilling to claim a life of her own, she withers and ultimately dies from her grief.

Cooper's efforts to demonstrate the cost of submission also extend to the level of character. Sergeant Dunham, Charles Cap, and Chingachgook court disaster because they are incapable of overcoming the weight of their own histories. Dunham, whose father "was a soldier before him," is utterly circumscribed by his military heritage and "looks at most things in this world over the barrel of his musket" (97). He resists commonsense revisions of British strategies, even when they are clearly called for, and imposes a military grid on every aspect of his life, including the marriage of his daughter. He has not "planned this marriage," he tells Natty, "without thinking it over, as a general does his campaign" (131). Cooper is somewhat sympathetic to Dunham's limitations—he has Natty excuse, for example, the Sergeant's preference for an army musket over the superior long rifle as the product of "long habit"—but he maintains, nonetheless, that the Sergeant's rigidity is inconsistent with his interests and those of his daughter (97).

Cap's subservience to his history is even more pronounced than that of the Sergeant. Despite ample evidence to the contrary, he refuses to believe that Lake Ontario requires different techniques of navigation and fails to adapt the maxims of ocean seamanship to his altered circumstances. When Jasper argues that he must anchor the vessel to avoid a wreck, he angrily dismisses him from the ship's deck. "Harkee, young man," he exclaims, "I've been a seafaring animal, boy and man, forty-one years, and I never yet heard of such a thing. I'd throw my ground tackle overboard before I would be guilty of so lubberly an act! . . . No man induces me to commit such a sin against my own bringing up" (248). "If I sink, I sink," he insists, "but d—e, I'll go down ship-shape and with dignity" (228).

Chingachgook, too, compromises his life and those of his companions by subordinating reason to tradition. Rather than avoiding a party of Iroquois, he launches a one-man attack against them. Natty's marksmanship saves his life, but when Chingachgook returns from his nearly fatal adventure, the scout chastises him. "Was it well done, Chingachgook," he asks, "to ambush a dozen Mingoes, alone! Killdeer seldom fails me, it is true; but the Oswego makes a distant mark, and that miscreant showed little more than his head and shoulders above the bushes, and an onpractysed hand and eye might have failed. You should have thought of this, chief; you should have thought of this!" Chingachgook responds by citing the burden of his ancestry. "The Great Serpent is a Mohican warrior," he insists, "he sees only his enemies, when he is on the war-path, and his fathers

have struck the Mingoes from behind, since the waters
began to run." Natty commends Chingachgook's devotion
to his blood but insists that "prudence as much becomes a
warrior as valor" (77). Tradition must, he argues, function
as a guide to conduct and not as its final arbiter.

Cooper's assault on subservience in *The Pathfinder* is
paralleled by an equally strenuous attack on unbridled originality. Each of the novel's three villains—Arrowhead,
Lieutenant Muir, and Captain Sanglier—has abandoned the
restraints of his heritage. Arrowhead, like Magua, is a traitor loyal only to himself. He has freed himself from his
history, but in the process, has become an outcast and a
moral leper. His death in the novel's concluding episode
assumes a didactic force. Arrowhead has himself been be-
trayed by Lieutenant Muir whom he ironically accuses of
"Too much lie" (422). When Muir responds to that charge
by attempting to strike him, Arrowhead plunges his knife
into the Lieutenant's chest and dashes into the forest, where
he is scalped by the faithful Chingachgook. Although by
killing Arrowhead, Chingachgook hastens the eventual
destruction of the tribes, his triumph over the renegade is a
victory for principle over expediency.

Muir's death at Arrowhead's hands is a singularly appropriate one in the terms of Cooper's moral universe. Muir
prides himself on his "auld bluid," but he surrenders his
heritage and his honor for a purse of double-louis. He has
been, Sanglier reports, the author of an anonymous letter
discrediting Jasper and has feigned an interest in Mabel to
sabotage the Sergeant's expedition. Confronted with the
evidence of Muir's deceit, Natty exclaims "What an awful
sinner! To plot, right and left, ag'in country, friends, and
the Lord!" "It isn't so much," he tells Jasper, that Muir

has disgraced his office, but that "he held a commission from God to act right, and to deal fairly with his fellow creatur's, and he has failed awfully in his duty" (426).

Captain Sanglier's treason is more subtle than that of Arrowhead and Muir. He never betrays the interests of France and, indeed, wins Natty's grudging respect as a "lawful and nat'ral enemy." But as an instigator of Indian ambushes and the paymaster of traitors, he violates principles which transcend national loyalties. Like Muir, Sanglier "has failed awfully in his duty." His leadership during Iroquois raids, Cooper writes, "exhibited the contradictory results of both alleviating the misery produced by this species of warfare, and of augmenting it, by the broader views and greater resources of civilization. In other words, he planned enterprises that, in their importance and consequences much exceeded the usual policy of the Indians, and then stepped in to lessen some of the evils of his own creating" (418). The personal consequences of that ambiguous service are considerable. Sanglier has acquired "a portion of the habits and opinions of his associates" and has, Natty insists, polluted his "white gifts" with red habits (419). Cold-blooded and selfish, he observes neither Christian nor savage restraints and becomes a frightening image of civilization's corruption in the wilderness. The legendary status he has acquired as a frontier wraith who leaves bloodshed in his wake is, Cooper tells us, unduly inflated. Sanglier's mythic status suggests, however, a level of cultural projection which Cooper exploits. Sanglier is terrifying, not simply because his Indian allies threaten the colonists' security, but because his alliance with savagery suggests both the fragility of civilized values and the psychic vulnerability of every man. Writing in 1840, Cooper is not primarily concerned with wilderness regression, but he employs Sanglier to address a more pressing cultural anxiety—the fear of unrestrained originality. Like Ishmael Bush, Sanglier is a version of American possibility. His liberation from the restrictive order of the Old World is not the source of a new beginning for mankind but an emblem of moral chaos and cultural decay.

Having framed the characteristic polarity of the Leatherstocking series, Cooper again imagines a marriage which suggests both the preservation of context and a departure from the past. Mabel and Jasper have demonstrated repeatedly their respect for traditional restraints. By rejecting three inappropriate suitors, each of whom asks her to violate the boundaries of principle and decorum, Mabel establishes the strength of her commitment to social order. Her refusal to become Arrowhead's squaw is phrased in conventional rhetoric—"To me it would be a lighter evil to be killed than to become the wife of an Indian"—but her defense of racial barriers is not advanced in the comfort of a drawing room (122). She is Arrowhead's prisoner and knows that the price of her integrity is torture and death. By virtue of his age and his five previous marriages, Lieutenant Muir is also an unworthy candidate for her hand, but his social position complicates Mabel's decision. As the daughter of a sergeant, she has been denied the position her education and talents merit, and finds herself in an untenable position. "While I am not," she confesses to Jasper, "good enough to be the wife of one of the gentlemen of the garrison, I think even you will admit . . . I am too good to be the wife of one of the common soldiers" (214). A marriage to Muir would resolve that dilemma and enable her to claim the rank she has been prepared to occupy, but Mabel's discipline overcomes her ambition. She is only briefly tempted by the prospect of "being raised above [her] station" (215) and concludes that she cannot marry a man who would come to regret that his wife was "the daughter of one so much his inferior as a sergeant" (215).

Natty's proposal demands an even more troubling choice. His age and frontier manners disqualify him as a suitable husband for Mabel. Moreover, she recognizes that a match with a man she "reverences as a daughter" would be "unwise—unnatural, perhaps" (271), but her judgment is impeded both by her father's wishes and by her promise to marry Natty in return for rescuing Sergeant Dunham from Indian captivity. While Muir's lack of personal honor fortified her resolve to reject an inappropriate marriage, she has no such grounds for repudiating her commitment to Natty. He has twice rescued her from certain death and has risked his life for her on several occasions. When Natty releases her from her pledge to him and asks her to choose a husband freely, Mabel's strength is sorely tried. She is bound to Natty by gratitude and filial devotion, but she recognizes that such a marriage would compromise her nature. After a moment's indecision, she tearfully rejects him and turns to Jasper Western.

Western's loyalties are tested as rigorously as Mabel's. Convicted without trial of treason and displaced as the captain of his own vessel, he has more than sufficient provocation for deserting the British cause. The inducements of vengeance and a French bounty do not, however, persuade him to sacrifice his honor. He continues to assist Sergeant Dunham and Charles Cap in the face of their suspicions and distinguishes himself in battle. Unlike Lieutenant Muir, Jasper resists the claims of self-interest and acts within the limits of his heritage.

But despite their uncompromising defense of tradition, Mabel and Jasper are capable of independent action. By rejecting Natty's proposal, Mabel strikes a blow against subservience and inscription. She rebels against Sergeant Dunham's tyranny and disappoints Natty, who has become her surrogate father. Jasper too is guilty of a kind of parricide. Natty is also his figurative father, and by taking Mabel as his bride, he disrupts their relationship and denies the power of paternal authority. More important, after his marriage, Jasper leaves Ontario and *The Scud* to begin a new life in New York City. That departure separates him from the other characters of the novel who are incapable of breaking with their pasts.

The narrative and thematic structure of *The Pathfinder*, is, then, entirely consistent with the earlier volumes of the Leatherstocking Tales. Cooper has apparently renewed the syntax he first elaborated in *The Pioneers* and reaffimed the series' historiographic scheme. But despite its similarities with *Mohicans*, *The Pathfinder* is not a reworking of that novel. Nor is it, like *The Prairie*, an attempt to review and buttress the assumptions of the preceding Tales. This is a novel which overturns Cooper's prior perspective. Jasper and Mabel's union differs significantly from those which conclude the other Leatherstocking Tales. In those novels, marriage is an unexamined trope which secures Cooper's vision of the dialectical thrust of American history. The weddings of Oliver Effingham and Elizabeth Temple, Duncan Heyward and Alice Munro, and Duncan Middleton and Inez de Certavallos defuse the social tensions Cooper examines and foreclose the cultural genesis he describes. By preserving context while disrupting entailment, they support Cooper's doubled vision of American history. Jasper and Mabel's marriage is also a formulaic device, but here Cooper is conscious of its conventionality. Their union is not a narrative convenience which sustains a precarious synthesis but is the central concern of Cooper's novel and the agency through which he reverses his point of view. Rather than renewing a paradoxical model of national time, Mabel and Jasper's marriage invalidates the prospect of American originality.

Cooper's revisionary intentions become apparent when he departs from his own prior practice of linking his marriages with the progressive course of national development and describes Jasper and Mabel's subsequent lives in more compromising terms. After a year's residence at Ontario, Mabel and Jasper return to New York where Jasper becomes a successful merchant and Mabel gives birth to "several youths" (468). Although Jasper's willingness to adopt a new career demonstrates his independence, his abandonment of *The Scud* is also a repudiation of his identity. Natty's response when Jasper announces his plans establishes the nature of that betrayal. "You, Jasper Western," he exclaims, "you, quit the lakes, the forests, and the lines, and this, too, for the towns and wasty ways of the settlements, and a little difference in the taste of the water. Have'n't we the salt-licks, if salt is necessary to you? And ought n't a man to be satisfied with what contents the other creatur's of God" (445). Jasper's destiny is even more remote from his gifts than Natty imagines, because it is as a merchant and not as an oceangoing seaman that he will earn his living.

In a novel centrally concerned with the violation of limits, Natty's reaction bears a considerable force, but Cooper's point is not that Jasper has erred in leaving the Great Lakes. His removal to New York is a necessary result of his marriage. As Natty himself admits, Mabel is unsuited to life on the unsettled frontier, and to remain at Ontario would require from Jasper a callous disregard for her welfare. Nor does Cooper describe their marriage as a mistake; Mabel's decision to wed Jasper is the optimal choice Cooper's narrative provides. Natty tells her that she deserves "the best husband America can produce," and within the limits of her possibilities, she achieves precisely what her merits demand (269). Rather, Cooper maintains that even the most prudent and intelligent lives can at best only repeat the constant pattern of man's history. Not as the progenitors of a new American beginning but as the heirs of human constancy, Mabel and Jasper rewrite the destinies of Cooper's young lovers. Jasper's career is ostensibly a productive one, but it lacks the resonance of Effingham's, Heyward's, and Middleton's achievements. Mabel, who has been an object of devotion and bloody rivalry, has become the wife of a merchant and the mother of his children. Their marriage does not bind a divided republic or generate "thriving villages" but yields, instead, the ordinary comforts of bourgeois respectability.[3]

Cooper reenforces the prosaic character of Mabel and Jasper's lives by glossing their marriage with a reference to

3 To some degree, Mabel and Jasper's limited achievement is the product of their heritage. Members of a lower social class than the other young lovers of the Tales, they cannot be entrusted with cultural leadership. But the absence of characters who might fulfill that role is itself an indication of Cooper's altered perspective in *The Pathfinder*.

Paradise Lost. Overcome by the pain they have caused Natty, "Jasper and Mabel sat," Cooper writes, "resembling Milton's picture of our first parents, when the consciousness of sin first laid its leaden weight on their souls" (457). This use of Adamic imagery might be perceived as evidence of misogyny:[4] it is true that Natty and Jasper fall from grace because a woman enters their wilderness paradise, and certainly Cooper's own youthful decision to resign his naval career on the Great Lakes to marry Susan De Lancey supports a reading of *The Pathfinder* as a nostalgic longing for the freedom of adolescence.[5] But such an analysis only partially exploits Cooper's allusion. Adam and Eve's originality as well as their sin is implicit in his referent. By resisting the authority of God, they effected a racial beginning which necessarily circumscribed both the possibilities and the limits of their heirs. All subsequent rebellion becomes, in the terms of Cooper's Edenic metaphor, recapitulation, evidence of human inscription. Mabel and Jasper displace two father figures but are powerless to overturn the inhibiting presence of their first parents. Their "sin" is finally a derivative act which documents their secondary status. Jasper's decision to surrender his life as a "Westerner" for the prosaic role of a merchant is, therefore, less a violation of his nature than it is a resignation of the illusion of originality. The American Revolution, which is a constant albeit a shadowy presence throughout *The Pathfinder*, is the principal analogue of Mabel and Jasper's diminished autonomy. The novel's postlapsarian motif redefines that cornerstone of America's freedom from the past and empties

4 See, e.g., Dekker, 166–69, and House, 310–13.
5 See Railton, 194–95.

it of its authority. Repetition and not difference is, Cooper suggests, the result of every War of Independence.

Natty's function in *The Pathfinder*'s Edenic parable also informs Cooper's historiographic intentions. As the patriarch against whom Jasper and Mabel rebel, he reenacts the role of Jehovah, the ultimate original, the source of beginnings. But just as God's options in Genesis are limited by Adam and Eve's free will, Natty's primacy is compromised when he frees Mabel from her promise to marry him. He no longer determines his future—if he could he would become Mabel's husband—but submits his life to her control. Rather than as the author of *The Pathfinder*'s denouement, he is now a character in the discourse Mabel creates. This abridgement of Natty's potency represents a significant departure from the earlier volumes of the Leatherstocking Tales. In those novels, Natty's liberation from the limits of history is an article of faith, a preexistent condition against which Cooper measures the progress of Natty's surrogate sons. America's departure from the past, which Natty's particularity secures, is a state which must be preserved and not a goal to be achieved. But in *The Pathfinder*, Cooper suggests that the autonomy he has attributed to Natty is itself an illusion. Natty's freedom from inscription, like that of Jehovah, evaporates when man appears in the Garden.

Mabel's, Jasper's, and Natty's independence is not the only casualty of the *Pathfinder*'s climax. Cooper's own originality is subsumed first by Milton, second by a biblical scribe, and finally by God himself. This pattern of concentric restriction invokes the most general of epistemological concerns, but what is of particular significance here is that Cooper has surrendered his authority as the framer of

American history. By acknowledging the derivative nature of both his characters' lives and his own imagination, he suggests that originality is not only unattainable but also unimaginable. There is, then, no need to contain American history within a narrative frame. The nation's beginning and ending, Cooper implies, were fully present when Europe first conceived the idea of a New World.

Cooper prepares his readers for the revisionary force of his conclusion by submitting Natty's character to the same deconstructive scrutiny he brings to bear on the conventional marriages of the first three Tales. Although at the time of *The Pathfinder*'s publication Natty was the most familiar character in American fiction, Cooper carefully reestablishes his heroic stature by contrasting his unerring vision and absolute morality with the fallibility of the novel's other figures. While the British soldiers at Ontario "battalion it about . . . in the forest, just as they did in their parks, at home" (51), Natty masters the "ways of the woods" and becomes a guide who finds his way "where there is no path" (18). But unlike Captain Sanglier, he fights "like a white man, and never like an Injin" (24). "Peace and marcy," he insists, are his "real gifts" (96). He never kills "unless it be plain that . . . death will lead to some good ind" (73).

Natty's humility serves as an insistent counterpart to the hubris of his companions. Rather than boasting of his exploits, he attributes his triumphs to the hand of God. He states, for example, that he was able to rescue Chingachgook during one of their adventures because the Almighty "led me to the only spot where execution could be done." "Many and many is the time," he says, "that my head would have been stripped of hair, skin and all, had'n't the Lord f'it of my side" (31). Throughout *The Pathfinder*, he excoriates his friends for trying to transcend their limitations. When Jasper pleads with him to miss his target during a shooting match so that he might distinguish himself in Mabel's eyes, Natty grants his request but exclaims, "What a creatur' is mortal man! He pines for things which are not of his gift, and treats the bounties of Providence lightly" (165). He refuses Cap's offer to go east with him to become a seaman as a violation of his gifts and explains his reluctance by relating a fable of the Delawares. A young brave, he tells Cap, once attempted to paddle his canoe to an island at the head of a waterfall, but despite his heroic efforts, he continued to lose ground until he was swept over the falls to his death. "Natur' has its limits," Natty concludes, and man's efforts to exceed them can only result in his destruction (286). Cooper summarizes Natty's character with a lengthy encomium.

> Ever the same, simple-minded, faithful, utterly without fear, and yet prudent, foremost in all warrantable enterprises, or what the opinion of the day considered as such, and never engaged in any thing to call a blush to his cheek, or censure on his acts, it was not possible to live much with this being . . . and not feel a respect and admiration for him, that had no reference to his position in life. . . . A disbeliever in the ability of man to distinguish between good and evil, without the aid of instruction, would have been staggered by the character of this extraordinary inhabitant of the frontier. His feelings appeared to possess the freshness and nature of the forest in which he passed so much of his time; and no casuist could have made clearer decisions in matters relating to right and wrong; and, yet, he was not without his prejudices, which, though few, and coloured by the character and usages of the individual, were deep-rooted, and almost formed a part of his nature. But the most striking feature about the moral organization of Path-

finder was his beautiful and unerring sense of justice. This noble trait, and without it no man can be truly great, with it no man other than respectable, probably had its unseen influence on all who associated with him, for the common and unprincipled brawler of the camp had been known to return from an expedition made in his company rebuked by his sentiments, softened by his language, and improved by his example. As might have been expected, with so elevated a quality, his fidelity was like the immovable rock. Treachery in him was classed among the things which are impossible; and as he seldom retired before his enemies, so was he never known, under any circumstances that admitted of an alternative, to abandon a friend. [134]

But even as he augments his legend, Cooper compromises Natty's virtue by exposing him to the urgings of "ambitious desire." Natty knows that he is unworthy of Mabel. As he tells Sergeant Dunham, he is "a poor hunter, and Mabel, I see, is f'it to be an officer's lady." Do "you think," he asks, "the gal will consent to quit all her beloved settlement usages, and her visitin's and church goin's to dwell with a plain guide and hunter, up, hereaway in the woods? Will she not in the ind crave her old ways, and a better man?" (131). Natty's instincts persuade him that "like loves like. The young prefar the young for companions, and the old the old" (132). "If I was younger, and more comely, now, as Jasper Western is," he muses, "there might be a chance—yes, then, indeed, there might be some chance" (131). When Dunham lists his marksmanship and his wilderness skills as talents that merit Mabel's love, Natty agrees with the Sergeant's assessment of his abilities but asks him what these gifts will "avail in gaining the good will of a tender-hearted young female" (130).

Nevertheless, Natty violates his fundamental principle

that every man must recognize his limitations. Despite his assertion that he will not "fly so much in the face of Heaven, as to try to become any thing else," he succumbs to temptation and asks Mabel to marry him (177). When she rejects that proposal with disbelief, he responds with a "convulsive" sorrow and pledges to "never think of [her], or any one else, again, in that way" (271). He agrees that such a marriage would be "agin natur'" and admits that he has "been on a false trail since we met." It is of "no avail," he sadly concludes, "to attempt to make the dove consort with the wolf" (276).

But Natty's repentance is short-lived. The Sergeant convinces him that Mabel's refusal is a conventional element of courtship and assures him that perseverance will win her hand. Once more, Natty protests that his "gifts are not altogether the gifts of Mabel Dunham," but he again betrays his principles, first, by accepting Mabel's promise to marry him if he rescues her father and, then, by proposing to her after he has freed her from that pledge (278). Natty prefaces this final proposal by contrasting his failings with Jasper's strengths. He is, he cautions Mabel, "fearful ignorant" and "altogether unfit for you," while Jasper is "frugal, industrious, and careful" (456) and "loves you as well as I do myself" (454). For Joel Porte, Natty's compromising appraisal of his merits suggests his desire to extricate himself from a courtship thrust on him by the Sergeant, but Natty's humility does not obscure his longing for Mabel Dunham.[6] However conscious Natty is of his unworthiness, there is, he says, "something pulling at my heart strings which seems hard to undo" (456). When Mabel chooses Jasper, Natty is "overcome with a sense of his loneliness"

6 Porte, 26.

and "his isolated condition in the world." Far from experiencing relief at Mabel's decision, he is left desolate and "without hope" (462). In his sorrow, he indicts his foolishness. "I have always known," he tells Mabel "that men have their gifts, but I'd forgotten that it did not belong to mine to please the young, and beautiful and l'arned. I hope the mistake has been no very heavy sin; and if it was, I've been heavily punished for it, I have" (458).

Heavy or not, Natty has sinned. Prior to meeting Mabel, he resisted every temptation. "Thrice," he tells Cap, "have I been sorely tried"—once when he found a French trapper's furs unattended in the wilderness, again when he thought to destroy the only rifle on the frontier that might rival Killdeer, and finally when he came upon a camp of sleeping Mingoes vulnerable to his knife (435).[7] On each of these occasions, Natty mastered his inclinations and sustained his innocence. But love blurs his judgment. On Mabel's first morning at the garrison, he chooses to stay by her side rather than accompanying a scouting party. He rationalizes his neglect of duty by arguing that the Iroquois have probably deserted the woods, and that, in any case, Chingachgook is present to assume his role. Natty's delinquency here is insignificant, but it is a prelude to more serious absences. He is aware, as he subsequently tells Mabel, that "the Sarpent is in his place, while I am not in mine"; still, he is incapable of returning to duty on the frontier (187).

Natty's prediction that his affection for Mabel "will be the spoiling of one of the best and most experienced scouts

7 See Terence Martin's provocative discussion of this passage in "From the Ruins of History: *The Last of the Mohicans*," *Novel* 2 (Spring 1969): 221–29.

on the lines" is an accurate one (190). Because he is not
"in his place," Arrowhead and Sanglier succeed in reaching
the garrison where they plot the betrayal of Dunham's
expedition with Lieutenant Muir. When Jasper learns that
an Indian and a French officer have been sighted conferring
near the fort, he tells Natty that had he "been outlying
that night, as usual, we should have secured one, if not both
of them." Natty's prior conduct has never called, "a blush
to his cheek, or censure on his acts," but he does blush at
Jasper's charge and admits that he is deserving of rebuke.
He explains his weakness by arguing that "we are all human, and all do wrong," but his consciousness of sin does
not deflect the consequences of his irresponsibility (208).

Natty does have one opportunity to compensate for his
error. As the Sergeant's scout, he leaves Mabel at Dunham's island base to accompany him in his attack against
the French. That assault is concluded successfully, but
rather than remaining with Dunham, he returns to the
island to insure Mabel's safety. Without Natty's guidance,
Dunham blunders into the ambush which costs him and his
men their lives. Natty recognizes that had he been with the
Sergeant's party their deaths could have been avoided. "I
do think," he tells Mabel, "if I had stayed with the boats,
this would not have come to pass! Other men may be as
good guides—I make no doubt they are; but then natur'
bestows its gifts, and some must be better than other some.
I dare say, poor Gilbert who took my place, has suffered
for his mistake" (385).

The practical effects of Natty's hubris are reenforced
by a corresponding psychic damage. His contentment van-
ishes as he longs to be young and handsome enough to please

Mabel, and he begins to worry that he will come to covet material things to make her comfortable. " 'Afore I knowd you," he tells Mabel, "the new-born babe did not sleep more sweetly than I used to could." His dreams, he reports, were full of his hunts and Indian pursuits; he awoke with pleasure to resume his calling. "Now," he admits, "I think no longer of any thing rude in my dreams; but the very last night we stayed in the garrison I imagined I had a cabin in a grove of sugar maples, and at the root of every tree was a Mabel Dunham, while the birds among the branches, sung ballads, instead of the notes that natur' gave, and even the deer stopped to listen. I tried to shoot a fa'an, but Killdeer missed fire, and the creatur' laughed in my face, as pleasantly as a young girl laughs in her merriment, and then it bounded away, looking back, as if expecting me to follow" (276).

Natty's dream is richly suggestive for a broad range of critical concerns, but its most fundamental effect is to reduce his stature further.[8] Natty's subconscious anxieties—and the vulnerability and impotence they record—humanize his character and redefine his role in Cooper's saga. For the first time in the Leatherstocking Tales, we see him as a confused and troubled figure whose aim is uncertain. Like the birds of his dream who sing ballads rather than the notes "natur' gave," Natty has been transformed. His identity, which was predicated upon his harmony with nature, has been compromised; his self-sufficiency has been lost. As H. Daniel Peck has argued, a recognition of the

8 See, e.g., Annette Kolodny, *The Lay of the Land: Metaphor as Experience and History in American Life and Letters* (Chapel Hill, N.C., 1975), 105–9, and David Noble, "Cooper, Leatherstocking, and the Death of the American Adam," *American Quarterly* 16 (1964): 424.

mutually exclusive relationship between women and the
woods, implicit in his dream, fragments Natty's consciousness and obscures the clarity of his vision.[9]

Susan Cooper tells us that Natty's romance in *The
Pathfinder* was the result of her father's whimsical desire
to imagine him in love.[10] But regardless of the lighthearted
spirit with which Cooper may have conceived the novel, he
directs Natty's vulnerability to a most serious purpose. In
surrendering Natty's difference and depriving him of his
immunity to weakness, Cooper abandons his defense of
American originality. The Natty of *The Pathfinder* is not
an icon of the nation's independence from history, nor is
he a guide who has realized a new beginning. The process
of initiation which Cooper's young heroes complete in the
other Tales is now Natty's burden. Through his courtship,
he passes from childhood to maturity and confronts the
contradictions and limitations inherent in his humanity.
Natty has not rewritten Adam's fate but has repeated his
fall.

And yet, Cooper does not conclude *The Pathfinder* by
describing Natty's grief but offers a coda which reinvokes
the context of *The Pioneers*. In the novel's final pages,
Mabel journeys in her middle years to the Mohawk Valley
where she sees Natty on a distant shore. When she inquires
about him, she is told that "he was the most renowned hunter of that portion of the State . . . a being of great purity of
character, and of as marked peculiarities, and that he was
known in that region of the country, by the name of Leatherstocking" (468). It is possible, of course, to argue that
by recalling Natty's role in *The Pioneers*, Cooper restores

9 Peck, 79–80.
10 Susan F. Cooper, 310.

Natty's innocence and originality. Free from the tempta-tions of sex and marriage, Natty, like Hester Prynne, has worked "out another purity than that which [he] had lost; more saint-like, because the result of martyrdom."[11]

But Cooper's tone here is as ironic as Hawthorne's. Natty's decision to separate himself from the corruption of Templeton affirms his autonomy and defines a cultural model. But in *The Pathfinder*, his retreat to the forests does not suggest rebirth but loss. Rather than maintaining his independence, Natty seeks an accommodation with the or-dinary. After he meets Mabel, he describes his originality not as a desirable condition but as a source of loneliness and isolation. He tells Mabel, for example, that "all other creatur's mate . . . and it was intended man should do so, too" (266). That assumption overturns Natty's commit-ment to a solitary life spent in harmony with nature and re-defines his virginity as an unnatural state. When he aban-dons the garrison for the wilderness, he embraces a damaged and incomplete existence, one which he knows is flawed. He says that at some future point he may master his feelings and visit Mabel and Jasper, but that moment never comes. He does not forget Mabel, indeed he sends her gifts of furs, but their reconciliation is unthinkable.

Unlike those of the first three Tales, the polarities of *The Pathfinder* are rigidly preserved. The worlds of wil-derness and civilization are irreconcilable: Jasper and Ma-bel cannot remain at Ontario; Natty must return to the forests. In the novel's concluding episode, Mabel stands on one side of the Mohawk and Natty on the other. They do not speak, the river is not bridged. But despite the gap

11 Nathaniel Hawthorne, *The Scarlet Letter* (Columbus, Ohio, 1962), 80.

which divides them, Natty and Mabel are both the victims of their common nature. Although they have risen in economic and social terms, Mabel and Jasper are enslaved by their history and have made no structural break from the past. Their prudent love demands that they marry and pursue a prosaic destiny. Natty's wilderness life and "marked peculiarities" distinguish him from ordinary men, but that difference implies a painful alienation. No more than Mabel and Jasper can he escape his nature to forge a new identity.

Natty and the Westerns have become in *The Pathfinder*'s conclusion inverted images of each other. Mabel and Jasper are insulated from loneliness but are bound by convention; Natty is free from, but longs for, context. Each of them shares a common pain whose source lies in their limitations. Natty dreams of a clearing in the woods where he and Mabel will live with Jasper and his wife. He will still scout and hunt; Jasper will continue to sail *The Scud*. When they return from their travels, their wives will greet them and "none," Natty believes, "could be happier than we four" (445). Like his analogous desire to become both Mabel's husband and her father, this fantasy of perfect contentment, of conjoined freedom and restraint, of male and female bonding is a fond but empty hope which Mabel's rejection of his proposal destroys. Mabel and Jasper too are denied the comforts of mediation. Mabel cannot both submit to, and rebel against, her father; she must choose between Jasper and Natty. Similarly, Jasper must resign *The Scud* and his friendship with Natty if he is to marry Mabel.

This failure to realize conflicting desires casts a gloom over *The Pathfinder*'s resolution. Natty loses Mabel and Jasper and recognizes his sterility. Cooper implies that Jasper will dream of *The Scud* as he conducts his business, and tells us that Mabel is overcome by melancholy and a "sleepless night" after she sees Natty across the Mohawk. The plenitude which has escaped them continues to haunt their lives. But more important, the necessity of a restrictive choice is itself only a fictional gambit. None of Cooper's characters are really free to choose. Mabel must disappoint Natty and marry Jasper; Jasper cannot remain at Ontario; and Natty can never transcend his isolation. This fatalism is at the heart of Cooper's historical perspective. The dream of a rooted originality which marked the earlier Tales has been discredited as a comforting fiction.

Like the characters of Hawthorne and James, whom they anticipate, Mabel, Jasper, and Natty are saddened but not diminished by the events of *The Pathfinder*. Freed from the illusions of childhood, they attain a maturity which paradoxically implies an admission of dependence. But rather than associating Cooper's perspective with those of Hawthorne and James, critics of *The Pathfinder* have generally located the novel against the backdrop of Cooper's mounting alienation from the main currents of his culture.[12] To some degree, *The Pathfinder* does recall the embittered pessimism of *Home As Found* (1838) and *The Monikins* (1835). In particular, Cooper's concern for the violation of context in the novel is consistent with his critique of contemporary American society.[13] But to read *The Pathfinder* as a further example of Cooper's assault on levelers,

12 Donald Ringe, e.g., argues in *James Fenimore Cooper* that the "fundamental purpose of the book is aligned with Cooper's social criticism in *Home As Found*. Cooper, Ringe maintains, employs the novel to insist "that social station is important at all levels of society" and to excoriate the contemporary state of American manners and values (81).

13 For discussions of the source and character of that alienation see Bewley; Meyers; Sundquist; Robert E. Spiller, *Fenimore Cooper: Critic of His Times* (New York, 1931); John F. Rosen, *The Social Criticism of Fenimore Cooper* (Berkeley, 1933); and Dorothy Waples, *The Whig Myth of Fenimore Cooper* (New Haven, 1938).

unprincipled journalists and politicians, Whiggish power brokers, and Anglophiles is to neglect its richness. Cooper does not call for a redirection of America's course in *The Pathfinder*, nor does he mourn the loss of past greatness, but he observes that from its inception, the nation has maintained a naïve conception of its possibilities. America's inability to achieve a separate destiny and effect a new beginning for mankind has not, he concludes, resulted from a failure of politics or social decorum but from the inescapable limitations of human nature.

A belief in history itself is the primary target of *The Pathfinder*'s energies. Like Hawthorne in "The Custom House Sketch," Cooper employs historiography to deny its validity. Far from resisting the erosions of time, he dismisses progress and decline as meaningless concepts. Against the force of his culture's confidence and the precedent of his own canon, Cooper indicts originality as a fantasy of childhood, an illusion unworthy of his generation.

~5~
An End in Our Beginning: The Myth of the Glimmerglass

The purpose of myth is to provide a logical model capable of overcoming a contradiction—an impossible achievement, if, as it happens, the contradiction is real.

> —*Claude Lévi-Strauss, "The Structural Study of Myth"*

The function of myth is to empty reality: it is, literally, a ceaseless flowing out, a haemorrhage, or perhaps an evaporation, in short a perceptible absence.

> —*Roland Barthes,* Mythologies

Dreams are but miserable guides when one has to determine about realities.

> —The Deerslayer

MYTH is history's antithesis. Where the historian confronts the disappointment of human longing and submits his accounts to the restrictions of the actual, the mythographer blurs complexity and claims for his narrative a timeless innocence and a transcendent clarity. The contradictions which frustrate the historian's efforts to organize his chronicle do not disrupt the fabric of myth. Indeed, as Claude Lévi-Strauss has argued, the essence of mythic consciousness is the erasure of conflict and the formulation of

159

impossible syntheses. Myth, Lévi-Strauss maintains, recognizes no boundaries and opposes its monolithic verities to the historian's halting attempts to comprehend change and continuity. But regardless of its appropriation of a natural status, myth does intersect with history at a significant point. By defining an ideal, myth reduces the temporal to a flawed realm of experience and historiography to a secondary activity forever anterior to, and dependent upon, the events it records. Because myth enshrines rather than explains, it establishes a model immune to revision limited only by the power of imagination.

History's opposition to myth is germane here because D. H. Lawrence's extremely influential reading of the Leatherstocking Tales is predicated on their difference. Lawrence describes the Tales as "a decrescendo of reality, and a crescendo of beauty," and argues that the series culminates in the "yearning myth" and "wish-fulfillment" of *The Deerslayer* (1841). In that "most fascinating Leatherstocking book," Lawrence finds the "myth of America"— the "gradual sloughing of the old skin" and the achievement of a "new youth"—fully realized.[1] Contemporary readers of the novel have generally conceded the accuracy of Lawrence's assessment and have adopted the terms of his metaphor. Cooper, we are told, sheds the old skin of the historical novelist and emerges in *The Deerslayer* as an American Homer, a transcendent poet who shapes a cultural ideal. Both the novel's fundamental difference from the rest of the series and the ahistorical character of its interests have become articles of critical faith, constants which

1 Lawrence, 154.

unite scholars of divergent methodologies and persuasions.[2]

The enduring power of Lawrence's perspective is easily understood. *The Deeryslayer*'s structure recalls the schematic pattern of legend and folklore. The mediator heroes and integrative marriages of the earlier Tales are absent; we are confronted instead with an irreconcilable battle for possession of the American continent. Cooper does not develop that conflict but establishes its terms in his initial episode. After he briefly describes the silent New York wilderness of 1740, he announces the presence of two travelers calling to each other in the forest. Their voices, he writes, "were in different tones, evidently proceeding from two men who were searching for their path."[3] As Marius Bewley has observed, Cooper's choice of language is deliberately portentous.[4] The two explorers, Hurry Harry March and Natty Bumppo, are diametrically opposed characters whose divergent responses to the virgin wilderness are metaphors for two trajectories of cultural possibility.

Stopping to recover their bearings, Hurry and Natty discuss a number of issues, disagreeing on each point they introduce. Their conversation ranges from the mundane to the profound but centers on two primary concerns: man's relation to nature and his obligations to his fellows. A handsome giant with massive strength but "a careless [and] slovenly manner," Hurry speaks for the unbridled freedom of the individual and the unbounded exploitation of the forests

2 Despite a growing shift away from mythologically based criticism, Cooper's readers continue to privilege Lawrence's assessment of the Tales. See, e.g., Peck, 186, and Railton, 209, 220.

3 James Fenimore Cooper, *The Deerslayer*, Darley-Townscend edition (New York, 1861), 14. Future references will be to this edition and will be cited by page number in the text.

4 Bewley, 88.

(18). The only limits he imposes on his trapping are pragmatic. He harvests all the furs he can transport and then returns to the settlements where he converts his pelts to gold. He defines his conception of social responsibility in similarly unrestrained terms. Like Ishmael Bush, he believes that "when we live beyond the law, we must be our own judges and executioners" (26). He rationalizes the violence which follows from that assumption as a convenience which saves "the magistrates trouble in the settlements" (19). Civil and moral sanctions have no place in Hurry's world view; the survival of the fittest is the only principle he espouses.

Natty lacks Hurry's "noble physique," but his "expression" is "that of guileless truth, sustained by an earnestness of purpose, and a sincerity of feeling" (17). Nature is not for him a source of wealth but a mirror of divine will, "an edication of itself to look upon" (33). "He sees God in the forest; hears him in the winds: bows to him in the firmament that o'ercanopies all; [and] submits to his sway in a humble belief of his justice and mercy." He is "in a word, a being who finds the impress of the Deity in all the works of nature, without any of the blots produced by the expedients, and power, and mistakes of man" (ix). Although he has earned the name Deerslayer through his prowess with a rifle, no one, he says, can "accuse me of killing an animal when there is no occasion for the meat or the skin. I may be a slayer, it's true, but I'm no slaughterer" (56). Human relations must, Natty concludes, be governed by the order reflected in the forests. "I know we live in the woods," he tells Hurry, "and are thought to be beyond human laws, but there is a law, and a law-maker, that rule across the whole continent. He that flies in the face of either, need not call me friend" (27). Natty's commitment to his principles is literally unshakeable. When Hurry throttles him for daring to oppose his will, Natty says that "you may shake until you bring down the mountain, but nothing beside truth will you shake from me" (27).

The conflict Cooper establishes between Hurry and Natty in *The Deerslayer*'s first chapter characterizes all of their subsequent relations. Hurry, we learn, is traveling to the Glimmerglass, the wilderness lake where all of the novel's action is set, to claim Judith Hutter as his bride. Enamored by her beauty, he has little regard for her substance. He is troubled by her flirtations with the officers of a British garrison, but he regards her nonetheless as a prize to be won and displayed in the settlements. Hurry approaches his courtship in the same ruthless manner in which he gathers his furs. If Judith has married in his absence, he will kill her husband and introduce her to "the pleasures of widowhood" (25). When Natty challenges the morality of such an act, Hurry ridicules his scruples. "If an inimy crosses my path," he asks, "will I not beat him out of it! Look at me—am I a man like to let any sneaking, crawling, skin-trader get the better of me. . . . And if a man *should* be found dead in the woods, who is there to say who slew him, even admitting the Colony took the matter in hand and made a stir about it?" (26). Natty is also on a matrimonial mission, but rather than pursuing his own interests, he has come into the region to help Chingachgook recover Hist, his kidnapped lover. While Hurry's quest is governed by Judith's beauty, Natty rejects so shallow a guide. "I would think no more of such a woman," he cautions Hurry, "but turn my mind altogether to the forest; *that* will not deceive you, being ordered and ruled by a hand that never wavers" (24).

The manner in which Hurry and Natty pursue their objectives further clarifies their opposition. Hurry agrees to join Tom Hutter, Judith's step-father, in a scalping expedition against the Hurons, because the British pay a bounty for Indian scalps, and because Hutter offers to exchange Judith for Hurry's assistance in the hunt. But Natty is convinced neither by Tom's argument that British policy sanctions scalping as a legitimate act of war nor by his contention that killing an Indian is a matter no more serious than trapping a beaver or shooting a deer. The scalp bounties are in Natty's judgment "a bad business" (48). "When the Colony's laws, or even the King's laws, run a'gin the laws of God," he tells Tom, "they get to be onlawful, and ought not to be obeyed" (49). Moreover, Natty maintains, Indians share a common human nature and may be slain only in "open and generous warfare" (19). Hurry and Tom are contemptuous of Natty's morality and attribute his resistance to his youth and his Moravian training. They demonstrate their "manhood" by ambushing women and children, while Natty preserves his virtue by killing his first brave in just and honorable battle.

As the novel's combat intensifies, Hurry continues to transgress the limits of both Indian and white convention. He violates Indian codes of honor by seeking scalps for profit rather than glory and denies the restraints of his own tradition by shooting women in the back and by refusing to observe a Huron flag of truce. He scorns Natty's decision to redeem a pledge he has given the Hurons as the "act of a madman or a fool" (438) and argues that he is not bound to deal fairly with the Indians because they have "neither souls nor names" (439). When Tom is killed and the security of his floating cabin is imperiled, Hurry abandons

Hutter's daughters and retreats to the garrison. He is, he says, "human enough to follow human natur', and that tells [me] to see the folly of one man's fighting a whole tribe" (428). By contrast, every aspect of Natty's conduct is governed by a rigorous morality. He fights only in accordance with his "gifts" and consistently resists the urgings of self-interest. Captured and then released on a furlough by the Hurons, he returns to their camp at the appointed hour even though he knows that to do so will result in torture and death. "A bargain is a bargain, though it is made with a vagabond," he tells the incredulous Hurry; his "word" demands that he honor the terms of his leave (427). Nor are Judith's professions of love sufficient to tempt him to abandon his principles. Despite her beauty and her offer to share the Glimmerglass with him, Natty rejects her as an inappropriate bride whose moral weakness and settlement inclinations are inconsistent with the demands of his nature. In any case, he warns, a marriage between them would be an unequal one. He is "too rude and ignorant" for Judith, and although "vanity is nat'ral," such hubris on his part "would surpass reason" (461).

Natty's conflict with Hurry is not in itself remarkable; his values are offset by a foil in each of the Leatherstocking Tales. But for the first time in the series, Cooper fails to imagine figures who might reconcile Natty's dispute with civilization. All of *The Deerslayer*'s characters are as remote as Hurry Harry from his virtue. The trappers who frequent the Glimmerglass are by Hurry's own admission, "headstrong and given to having their own way, without bethinking 'em of other people's rights and feelin's" (28). Taken "as a body," Natty tells Judith, " 'arth don't hold a set of men more given to theirselves and less given to God and the law" (456). Although some of the trappers do assist Hutter in building his home in the middle of the Glimmerglass, other members of their community have driven him to that expedient by looting and burning his cabin.

The British soldiers of the novel practice a less crude but equally malignant villainy. The European officers of the earlier Leatherstocking Tales were, despite their arrogance, generally honorable men, but, as A. N. Kaul has observed, they have been replaced in *The Deerslayer* by "a heartless band of elegant seducers."[5] Preying on the women of the frontier, they toast the pleasures of bachelorhood and celebrate their reputation as a regiment of merry rakes. Only once in the course of the novel do we see them involved in an activity other than seduction. In one of Cooper's concluding episodes, a detachment under the command of Captain Warley attacks the Huron camp where Natty is held prisoner. They release him from bondage, but do so in a needlessly brutal fashion which Cooper contrasts both with Natty's self-discipline and with the more limited and tradition-bound violence of the Indians. Sweeping into the encampment, Warley's troops indulge themselves in wanton bloodshed. "All of the women," Cooper reports, "and some of the Huron girls, had fallen by the bayonet; either in the confusion of the *mêlée*, or from the difficulty of distinguishing the sexes, where the dress was so simple. Much the greater portion of the braves suffered on the spot. A few had escaped, however, two or three had been unharmed. As for the wounded, the bayonet saved the surgeon much trouble" (573). Warley's callous response to this carnage is as disturbing as the violence he sponsors. He is indifferent

5 A. N. Kaul, *The American Vision: Actual and Ideal Society in Nineteenth-Century Fiction* (New Haven, 1963), 128.

to the burial of the battle's victims, preferring "attendance on Miss Judith Hutter" to service "on a point of the lake, however romantic the position or brilliant the victory" (571). He extends only cursory attention to his own wounded and jests that a soldier with a terminal stomach wound will find the taking of nourishment "rather inconvenient." His principal concerns are lost sleep from "being up two nights *de suite*" and his plans for parading Judith at the fort (572).

Cooper describes the Hutter family in more detail and with greater complexity, but he continues to preserve the gulf which separates Natty from the novel's other characters. A pirate and freebooter—reputedly a colleague of Captain Kidd—Tom Hutter has fled an eastern hangman for the anonymity of the wilderness. The natural harmony of that setting has not, however, had a regenerative effect on his character. When the British offer a bounty for Indian scalps, he returns to his former calling with undisguised relish. Arguing that "money 'arned in this way is . . . as likely to pass as money 'arned in trapping and hunting," Hutter proposes an attack on the Huron camp, directed primarily against defenseless victims. "If there's women, there's children" he tells Hurry, "and big and little have scalps; the Colony pays for all alike" (89). The wilderness has not elevated his spirit as it has Natty's, but has accelerated his degeneration. "Old Tom's human natur'," Hurry observes, "is not much like other men's human natur', but more like a muskrat's human natur', seeing that he takes more to the ways of that animal than to the ways of any fellow creatur' " (21).

Judith and Hetty are more sympathetic characters than their father, but they too are remote from Natty's values.

Judith comes to repent the vanity which has sullied her reputation and imagines a life of recovered innocence as Natty's wife. Natty, however, doubts the strength of her resolve. "These are brave words," he says of Judith's promise to adopt a new standard of virtue, "but do you think that the feelins' would keep 'em company, did the ch'ice actually lie afore you." (460). Natty's skepticism is well founded. Disappointed by his rejection of her proposal, she abandons her good intentions and becomes Warley's mistress. Judith's sister, Hetty, is "a pure, excellent, sinless creature," but her mental deficiencies impede her judgment. She is naïve enough to believe that she can alter Indian nature by reading to the Hurons from the Bible and trusts implicitly in the innate goodness of man. Utterly incapable of recognizing evil, she is vulnerable to its force. Natty warns her that her optimistic view of human nature "may do among the missionaries, but would make an oncertain life in the woods" (412). He is incapable, however, of arming her with his militant virtue and must consign her to the simplicity of her private universe. No more than Judith can she share Natty's world view.

Cooper's choice of setting in *The Deerslayer* also supports a Lawrentian reading of the novel. Departing from the precedent of the earlier Tales, Cooper does not locate his narrative within the flux of history but evokes a sense of timelessness consistent with the world of myth. The progressive course of settlement and the emergence of "thriving villages" cease to interest Cooper in *The Deerslayer*. Rather than looking forward to describe the transformation of the wilderness, he reverses his perspective to recall "the earliest days of colonial history," a "remote and obscure" period, lost in the "mists of time" (13). "A bird's-eye view of the whole region east of the Mississippi," he writes, "must then have offered one vast expanse of woods ... dotted by the glittering surfaces of lakes, and intersected by the waving lines of rivers" (15). The national "infancy" which *The Deerslayer* records is both pre- and ahistorical in character. Cooper anticipates the eventual advance of settlement, and indeed, he tells us in his preface that the Glimmerglass has become Lake Otsego, the setting of his boyhood home. But the establishment of Cooperstown is outside *The Deerslayer*'s frame; change is rigorously excluded from its scope. "Centuries of summer suns" have passed without altering the forests. Time there is measured only by the circular "rounds of the seasons" (15). When, in *The Deerslayer*'s concluding chapter, Natty and Chingachgook return to the Glimmerglass fifteen years after the events of the novel, the lake is still unmarred by human presence. "It was probable," Cooper tells us, that the region "had not been visited since the occurence of the final scene of our tale" (596). Lost in the midst of this "solemn solitude," the Glimmerglass is "a world by itself" (157) "hermetically" sealed against intrusion (83). Unmapped and unnamed by the colonial legislature, it is less a physical setting than it is a state of mind, a realm of the imagination "sacred to nature" (87).

Like mythic discourse, which characteristically deals with origins, *The Deerslayer* centers on the question of beginnings.[6] Its setting, of course, suggests an American genesis. "The hand of man," Cooper writes, "had never yet defaced or deformed any part of this native scene"(33).

6 See Martin's discussion of the importance of beginnings in *The Deerslayer* in particular, and in the Leatherstocking series in general, in "Beginnings and Endings in the Leatherstocking Tales."

"Not a tree," Natty remarks, has been "disturbed even by redskin hand, as I can discover, but everything left in the ordering of the Lord" (34). All of *The Deerslayer*'s characters are themselves involved in a quest for a beginning: Natty and Chingachgook are on their first warpath; Tom Hutter has settled at the Glimmerglass to escape his history; Judith hopes to launch a new destiny by marrying Natty; the officers of the British garrison are the agents of Europe's search for a New World. Extending the Adamic metaphor of *The Pathfinder*, Cooper sets *The Deerslayer* in a virgin wilderness free from "dangerous serpents" (182). There Judith longs for a protector "to turn this place into a Garden of Eden" and tempts Natty with a sexual initiation which will compromise his innocence (408).

That enticement is the last in a series of tests which challenge Natty's immunity to human weakness. He has resisted Hurry and Tom's urgings to join their bounty hunt, refused a Huron offer to spare his life if he will agree to marry a squaw and join their tribe, and rejected Judith's plea to default on his promise to return to the Huron camp. By overcoming each of these temptations, Natty earns the title "King of the Woods" and becomes worthy of embracing his wilderness "bride" (422). The mythic aspect of Natty's trials is an obvious one, but Cooper does not depend on that motif to secure his character's legendary status. When Natty kills his first Indian, Cooper explicitly identifies him as a national archetype. In that episode, Natty is fired on from ambush, but he refuses to take advantage of his foe and permits him to rearm. Insisting that "war isn't needfully massacre," he attempts to reason with the Indian and avoid bloodshed. Only when the brave fires a second time, does Natty take his life. He then cradles the dying Indian in his arms and assures him that his principles prohibit him from taking his scalp. "White I was born," he tells him, "and white I will die, clinging to color to the last, even though the King's Majesty, his governors, and all his councils, both at home and in the colonies, forget where they come from and where they hope to go" (130). In acknowledgment of that virtue, the dying Indian gives Natty his benediction and names him "Hawk-eye." Such, Cooper concludes, "was the commencement of a career in forest exploits that afterward rendered this man, in his way, and under the limits of his habits and opportunities as renowned as many a hero whose name has adorned the pages of works more celebrated than legends simple as ours can ever become" (120).[7]

Lawrence's view of *The Deerslayer* as a "yearning myth" is reenforced by biographical as well as textual evidence. *The Pathfinder* and *The Deerslayer* follow from a decade of political and social disaffection. Angered by libelous reviews of his work and disgusted by the mendacity of American culture, Cooper announced his retirement as a novelist in 1834 and devoted himself to travel writing and social criticism. He returned to fiction four years later with the publication of *Homeward Bound* (1838) and *Home As Found* (1838), but he did not abandon his attack on American mores. In both of those works, and in all of his subsequent novels, Cooper renews his critique of contemporary values by setting his narratives in a world dominated by expediency and self-interest. But while in the 1830s, he had hoped that his social views would prompt thoughtful debate, the antagonism which greeted his writing had, by

7 See Ivor Winters's description of Natty's initiation as a crucial component of Cooper's "great national myth" in *In Defense of Reason* (Chicago, 1974), 187–90.

1840, led him to despair of an audience. Indeed, in his general preface to the Leatherstocking Tales, he suggests that "if all of the facts could be ascertained, it is probable the result would show that, all those (in America, in particular) who have read the first three books of the series, not one in ten has a knowledge of the existence even of the last two" (vii). This context provides, of course, ample grounds for reading *The Deerslayer* as a work in which Cooper repudiates a corrupt and disappointing reality and resorts to an escapist fantasy. It may well be argued that by returning to the setting of *The Pioneers*, Cooper imaginatively obliterates the world of that novel and advances in its stead a vision of a timeless wilderness impervious to change. Cooper's preface is consistent with such an analysis. Having noted critical objections to his "favourable picture of the redman," he defends "the privilege of all writers of fiction, more particularly when their works aspire to the elevation of romances, to present the *beau ideal* of their characters to the reader. . . . Such criticism would have deprived the world even of Homer" (x).

Lawrence's analysis of *The Deerslayer* is, then, a well-buttressed position. The conclusions he derives from his reading of the novel are, however, seriously flawed. He is right when he describes *The Deerslayer* as the culmination of the Leatherstocking series, but he underestimates the intricacy of its relation to the preceeding volumes of the Tales. Despite their engagement of the historical world, the first three Tales are predicated on a fantasy. In each of these novels, Cooper designs a temporal model which effects the illusory synthesis Lévi-Strauss defines as the object of myth. America, Cooper tells us, is both free from, and bound to, the past. Its future is simultaneously inde-

pendent of constraint and contained by precedent. By ex-
iling Natty in his final chapters, Cooper appears to privilege
reality over romance, but in fact, the marriages he describes
are themselves the product of a mythic consciousness. The
plenitude they realize, their reconciliation of freedom and
restraint, is a comforting fiction which discharges cultural
anxiety and achieves a false sense of closure.

In *The Pathfinder*, Cooper inverts his narrative strategy. Rather than surrendering his conclusion to Mabel and
Jasper, he enshrines Natty as a legendary hunter and "a
being of great purity."[8] His isolation on the far shore of the
Mohawk undermines the integrative power of the Western's marriage and reduces the primacy of the world they
occupy. But, as I have suggested, Cooper's tone in *The
Pathfinder*'s conclusion is strongly ironic. The myth of a
rooted originality, like Natty's dream of a cabin in a clearing, is overturned, and we are left with a melancholy vision
of human limitation. *The Deerslayer* extends the implications of *The Pathfinder*'s denouement by immediately ceding to Natty the mythic position he occupies in the final
passages of that novel. An idealized image of what America
might have become, Natty is clearly the product of a dream.
But Cooper does not embrace that illusion. He recognizes
it for what it is—a powerful fantasy and an eternal longing
consistent with the historiographic paradigm of the first
three Tales.

The influence of Lawrence's reading of the Tales has
been such, however, that Cooper's detachment from the
myth he creates has gone largely unnoticed. Rather than
contesting Lawrence's assumptions, Cooper's critics have
explored their implications. Marius Bewley, A. N. Kaul,

8 *The Pathfinder*, 468.

and R. W. B. Lewis have, for example, stressed Cooper's didactic intentions. Bewley argues that in *The Deerslayer* Natty "remains a perpetual possibility of perfection to the American imagination—and a perpetual reproach." His refusal to seek an accommodation with civilization demonstrates for Bewley Cooper's commitment to an ideal conception of American potential and gives voice to the "love and revulsion" he felt for his nation.[9] Kaul adopts a similar position by describing the novel as a source of "cultural renewal and endless inspiration." However idealistic it may be, Natty's renunciation of the corruption of the settlements enacts "a moral function which is constructive because it is critical."[10] In *The American Adam*, Lewis is even more explicit about Natty's regenerative role. "With all of the ardour of a declining conviction," he writes, Cooper turns in *The Deerslayer* from "his historic world" to the "invulnerable world of myth" and frames in Natty's character "an enduring model for the actual."[11]

A second group of readers adhere more closely to the spirit of Lawrence's essay and maintain that Cooper's purposes are escapist and not instructive. Locating the Leatherstocking Tales within what he describes as an anarchistic tradition of American letters, Irving Howe argues that like Melville, Twain, and Mailer, Cooper refuses to embrace a less than ideal world and spurns social engagement for "a wistful ballet of transcendence." In "their bitterness with the social reality and their tacit recognition that they cannot really affect its course," he concludes, "American writers seek to get around or to 'transcend' the intractability of

9 Bewley, 107.
10 Kaul, 118.
11 Lewis, 103.

what they encounter."[12] Quentin Anderson too rejects a didactic reading of *The Deerslayer*. "Although," he remarks, "Cooper's myth begins as the myth of the ideal citizen, it does not end that way. Leatherstocking is not the ideal citizen; he offers an alternative to civilization." *The Deerslayer* is, Anderson continues, "a youthful reverie" which records a "loving self-absorption in the spectacle of one's own virtuosity" and celebrates a hero who "reads himself out of society."[13] More simply, Thomas Philbrick characterizes *The Deerslayer* as an attempt to "retreat from the oppressive reality of the here and now."[14]

Both of these critical positions have the effect of reducing the complexity and the coherence of Cooper's vision in the Leatherstocking series. Of the two, a didactic reading of the novel is more obviously problematic. It is true that in the first three Tales Cooper exploits Natty's function as a guide. By directing the growth of Oliver Effingham, Duncan Heyward, and Duncan Middleton, Natty points the way for the dialectical development of American culture. The young heroes of these novels profit from his example and successfully transmit his values within a social context. But in *The Pathfinder*, Cooper firmly refutes Natty's ability to serve as "an enduring model for the actual." The gulf he creates between the Westerns and Natty in his final chapter is absolute; the worlds of wilderness and civilization are thoroughly disjunctive. Rather than moving toward a closer relationship with Natty, as Duncan Heyward does, Jasper breaks their bond by abandoning Ontario for

12 Irving Howe, *The Decline of the New* (New York, 1963), 93–111.
13 Quentin Anderson, "Introduction," *The Deerslayer* (New York, 1962), 9.
14 Thomas Philbrick, *James Fenimore Cooper and the Development of American Sea Fiction* (Cambridge, Mass., 1961), 127.

a merchant's office. Natty's impotence is even more pronounced in *The Deerslayer*. In none of the other Tales is
he so insistent on instructing his companions. He lectures
each of them in turn and charts for them a certain path to
virtue. But his efforts are entirely without effect. Hurry and
Tom continue to scalp Indians, Judith fails to amend her
conduct, and Hetty is incapable of even understanding Natty's advice. Natty himself is finally convinced of the futility
of reforming his friends. "We must take things as they are,"
he tells Chingachgook, "and not as we want 'em to be"
(471).

Cooper does not permit us to attribute the failure of
Natty's instruction to the particular weaknesses of his characters, but demands that we locate their recalcitrance within
a broader context. When Natty learns that the Hutter
family is "off on a v'y'ge of discovery" aboard their boat
The Ark, he repeats for Hurry's benefit the Moravian account of the flood (40). By introducing that reference, Cooper links the European settlement of America with Noah's
landfall at Mount Ararat. The failure of Noah's descendants to realize the potential of the new world which
stretched before their eyes is clearly offered as an allegory
for the course of American history. Incapable of profiting
from experience, men have repeated in the New World the
errors of the Old. Tom Hutter's *Ark* is a source not of regeneration but of bloodshed and corruption. He is as much
a member of "a fallen race" as is Chingachgook; regardless
of his context, rebirth is beyond his grasp (31). To argue,
then, as Donald Ringe does, that Cooper concludes the
Leatherstocking saga with "a final note of affirmation" is to
misinterpret Cooper's intent.[15] Far from identifying Natty

15 Ringe, *James Fenimore Cooper*, 84.

as a figure of inspiration, Cooper insists on the constancy of human error.

He further supports that assumption by attaching considerable metaphoric weight to the sea chest Tom Hutter has brought with him into the forests. Standing at the center of his cabin, in much the same way as that cabin stands in the center of the Glimmerglass, and the lake stands at the center of the novel's forest terrain, Hutter's chest anchors Cooper's deterministic vision of human destiny. Its significance first becomes clear when Tom is captured by the Hurons, and Natty and Judith open it in hopes of finding something of value to barter for his release. They uncover a set of chessmen which the Indians accept in trade for Hutter, but they also unearth Tom's history—a buccaneer's flag and a wanted poster identify him as Tom Hovey, a notorious pirate. It is not, however, only Hutter's past which is buried in the chest, but Judith's and Hetty's as well. By reading a packet of her mother's letters, Judith learns that she and her sister are not Hutter's children but are the illegitimate offspring of a British officer.

The revelations of the chest function on four distinct levels, each of which suggests a static conception of human potential. Initially, its contents document the endurance of Hutter's barbarity. The Glimmerglass has afforded him a new beginning, but he has squandered that opportunity by repeating his crimes. He has cheated the hangman, but his destiny is essentially unchanged. Trapped in his seemingly impregnable cabin, he is scalped by the Hurons and left to suffer an agonizing death. On a second level, Judith discovers that her mother's sin was not the product of a momentary weakness. A letter from Judith's grandmother makes clear that she has ignored her mother's repeated warnings and prolonged her disastrous affair. Even after the consequences of that liaison have destroyed her happiness, Judith's mother does not reform, but chooses instead to marry the pirate Hovey.

Judith recognizes too that her own life has closely paralleled her mother's. She recalls that she has also resisted maternal pleas to avoid temptation and has sacrificed her virtue for scarlet coats and empty flattery. As she reads her father's letters, "her hand shook," Cooper writes, and "cold shivers again passed through her frame as she discovered a few points of strong resemblance between these letters and some that it had been her own fate to receive" (446). Cooper's point is not simply that Judith has re-enacted her mother's sin, but that even in the face of that example she is incapable of change. Despite her pledge to abandon the course that led to her mother's disgrace, she subsequently weakens and also becomes the mistress of a British officer.

Finally, the treasures of Tom Hutter's chest suggest that the history of corruption which they record will be recapitulated in the wilderness. The elegant clothing, the ivory chessmen, the silver-inlaid pistols, and the nautical sextant Judith and Natty find in the trunk are singularly out of place in the wilderness, but their appeal is undiminished. When Judith responds with "rapture" to her mother's gown, Natty cautions her that the dress cannot possibly be worn in the forest, and that in any case, it is an inappropriate garment for "Thomas Hutter's darter" (230). But as she models the dress, Natty is transfixed by her beauty and exclaims with "wonder and pleasure" that "never did eyes of mine gaze on as glorious a lookin' creatur' as you be yourself, at this very moment" (228). Chingachgook is as taken with Judith's father's scarlet coat as she is with her mother's dress. Although his appearance in the jacket is "ludicrous," Chingachgook preens before a mirror and wishes that "he could be seen by [Hist] in his present improved aspect" (227). "Nothwithstanding all his trained self-command," Cooper remarks, "the splendor of the vestment was too much for the philosophy of an Indian" (226).

Despite their uselessness, the chessmen hypnotize Chingachgook and the Hurons. "Elephon buy whole tribe," Chingachgook says of the ornamented rooks, "buy Delaware almost" (242). Natty's conviction that the ivory pieces are idols demonstrates his naïveté, but his mistake accurately predicts the fervor with which the bellicose tradition the chessmen depict will be renewed on the frontier. Hutter's dueling pistols, Cooper surmises, had once been the property of an officer "impressed with the ways of London," but he recognizes that they will be employed as readily in the New World as in the Old. At first, Natty scorns them as foolish novelties, but he cannot resist challenging Chingachgook to a test of marksmanship. Their contest is a friendly one, but it is predicated on a desire for mastery. When Chingachgook badly misses his target, Natty ridicules his effort. "Well done Sarpent," he laughs, "you've hit the lake and that's an explite for some men! . . . Now stand back and let us see what white gifts can do with a white we'pon" (251). As Natty fires his gun, it explodes in his hand, bringing the game to a nearly fatal conclusion. Like the rest of the contents of Hutter's chest, the dueling pistols symbolize the dangers and the constancy of man's vanity and argue against the prospect of historical departure.

A reading of *The Deerslayer* as an exercise in wish fulfillment is considerably more persuasive. As H. Daniel

Peck has convincingly argued, it is a book "touched by
reverie."[16] Its power lies in its ability to engage our own
longings for escape; it awakens the child within all of us.
Cooper's own attraction to the image of a pristine lake belted
by forests is unmistakable. He invests enormous emotional
energy in *The Deerslayer*'s landscape and is deeply moved
by the dream he unfolds. To some degree, the Glimmerglass's resonance for Cooper results from his boyhood on
its shores, but the sources of its appeal run deeper than
memory. As Cooper describes Natty's romance with the
lake and the woods, he evades not only a difficult present
but limitation and restraint as well. But it is important to
distinguish between Cooper's attraction to the world of the
Glimmerglass and his commitment to the fantasy it embodies. Like Natty, Cooper recognizes that "dreams are but
miserable guides when one has to determine about realities," and it is realities that Cooper addresses in *The Deerslayer* (443). The possibilities which Natty's final departure for the wilderness open have already been foreclosed
in the other volumes of the Tales. His dispossession in *The
Pioneers*, his disappointment in *The Pathfinder*, and his
death in *The Prairie* are fully present in *The Deerslayer*'s
text. The westward extension of settlement cannot be
slowed, and there are no territories toward which Natty may
safely flee. Moreover, Cooper recognizes the fatal solip-
sism implicit in Natty's autonomy. By inverting the matrimonial plot of *The Pathfinder*, by casting Judith Hutter
rather than Natty as a spurned suitor, Cooper reminds us
that Natty's freedom will lead to isolation and despair.

   Rather than opposing a timeless innocence to the erosions of history, Cooper embarks on a more dispassionate

16 Peck, 161.

and self-conscious enterprise. Dismissing the doubled vision of the first three Tales, he suggests that both originality and progress are unattainable ends. Men forever seek the same objectives and confront the same limits. The very dream he records in *The Deerslayer* is an emblem of that constancy. Natty's idyllic escape from time may be "the myth of America," but it is also an expression of a universal longing, implicit among other places in the biblical account of the Flood, in the European colonization of America, and in the "more celebrated" works which Natty's adventures recall. That is not to deny the power Cooper accords that dream but is, rather, to suggest that he does not renew its terms in an uncritical manner. As tempting as it may be to describe *The Deerslayer* as an Adamic myth, and to agree with Joel Porte that Natty "makes a pact with the devil" and with him excludes "women from the virgin forest," such a reading invokes the wrong biblical context.[17] Noah's repetition of Adam's fall is more central to Cooper's purpose, as is the example of Job. Cooper describes that book of the Bible as Judith's mother's favorite text and has Hetty read from it to her dying father. Job's resignation in the face of his impotence provides an important gloss for the novel and brings us to a clearer sense of Cooper's perspective.

And yet, *The Deerslayer*'s scriptural subtext is only a secondary concern. The primary issue here is the extent of Cooper's commitment to Natty as a cultural ideal. There can be no question about Cooper's unqualified admiration for his character. By successfully resisting the hypocrisy of the "King's Majesty" and the savagery of the Hurons and the borderers, Natty attains a level of moral perfection.

17 Porte, 28.

But his innocence is achieved entirely through negation. His example does not provide a model which can inform the life of a culture but suggests a strategy for avoiding an immersion in its currents. Irving Howe would argue that sterility *is* the ideal Cooper offers his readers. Flee! Transcend! Escape! But Cooper's sophistication, I would argue, is of a higher order than Howe is willing to admit. He does propose a model of cultural possibility in *The Deerslayer*, but that prospect is never realized. When Judith offers herself to him, Natty has an opportunity to satisfy the longings which trouble him in *The Pathfinder*. A cabin in a clearing is within his grasp; Cooper extends for a moment an image of realized plenitude. By marrying Judith, Natty might realize the promise of the New World and reconcile the conflicting urges of independence and context. But he remains "a man without a cross" and is trapped in the world of childhood.[18] Cooper invokes the dialectical resolutions of the first three Tales only to undercut their force. American history, he concludes, is a contradiction in terms. There is only human history, and insofar as history implies progress toward an ideal, it is itself a fiction.

Unlike those of the first three Leatherstocking Tales, *The Deerslayer*'s narrative is circular rather than linear. Rather than progressing toward a marriage and the resolution of its narrative tensions, *The Deerslayer* ends where it begins, with a description of the unsettled wilderness of New York State. Natty and Chingachgook have returned fifteen years later to the Glimmerglass where they find that

> all was unchanged; the river still rushed through its bower of
> trees; the little rock was wasting away by the slow action of

18 See Peck on the purely formal nature of Natty's initiation (80) and on his arrestment in childhood (70–80).

the waves in the course of centuries; the mountains stood in
their native dress, dark, rich and mysterious; while the sheet
glistened in its solitude a beautiful gem of the forests. [595]

Turning the point of the lake, they discover only the ruins
of Hutter's cabin. "The storms of winter," Cooper writes,

> had long since unroofed the house, and decay had eaten into
> the logs. All the fastenings were untouched, but the seasons
> rioted in the place, as if in mockery at the attempt to exclude
> them. The palisades were rotting, as were the piles, and it was
> evident that a few more gales and tempests would sweep all
> into the lake and blot the building from the face of that magni-
> ficent solitude. The graves could not be found. Either the
> elements had obliterated their traces, or time had caused those
> who looked for them to forget their position. [596]

Cooper's decision to close *The Deerslayer* with an image
of decay is not an indication of either presumption or despair. He does not introduce Hutter's abandoned cabin to
affirm the triumph of virtue over vice or to vicariously destroy a civilization he had come to despise. His purpose is
the revision of his earlier meliorism. Our endings, he suggests, are present in our beginnings. Although in the novel's
final sentence, Cooper maintains that "happily for human
nature, gleanings of that pure spirit in whose likeness man
has been fashioned, are to be seen, relieving its deformities,
and mitigating, if not excusing its crimes," he concludes
that "we live in a world of transgressions and selfishness
and no pictures that represent us otherwise can be true"
(597). The progressive assumptions of the earlier Tales
are abandoned as the products of a naïve perspective. Cooper offers us a dream of transcendence and originality, but
however drawn he may be to Natty's belief that "all is con-

cord in the forest" (286), he agrees with Tom Hutter that "the consciences in the settlements [are] pretty much the same as they are out here in the woods" (115).

The spirit of resignation which pervades *The Deerslayer* is perhaps best exemplified in Cooper's consideration of names and naming. There are two kinds of designation in the novel—names given at birth and those earned or claimed in life. The former are unreliable gauges of identity. March is an appropriate name for a member of civilization's advance guard, and Hutter adequately describes Tom's status in the wilderness, but Natty's humble family name is disjunctive with his stature as the "King of the Woods." Hetty's and Judith's names, which their parents chose from the Bible, also belie their characters. Unlike the biblical Esther, Hetty is not a savior of her people but a pathetic innocent whose attempt to rescue her family and friends from the Hurons leads only to her death. Judith's distance from her namesake is even more pronounced. The biblical Judith scrupulously observed Mosaic law and resisted the temptations of Holofernes, but Judith Hutter violates moral sanctions and succumbs to the flattery of the garrison.

The "sobriquets" of Cooper's characters are more consistent with their natures. Each of Natty's Indian names defines an aspect of his identity. He has been called Straight-tongue because he "was not given to lying," Pigeon because he "was quick of foot," Lap-ear because he "partook of the sagacity of a hound," and Deerslayer because he "could keep a wigwam in ven'son" (69). The name he earns in this novel—Hawk-eye—is a measure of his marksmanship and moral precision. The novel's other characters have equally descriptive nicknames. "Hurry Skurry" epitomizes Harry March's reckless manner, just as "The Muskrat" defines Tom Hutter's bestial nature. Chingachgook is called the "Big Serpent" because of his "wisdom, and prudence, and cunning." Judith's name, "The Wild Rose," establishes both her beauty and her lack of discipline, while "The Drooping Lilly" suggests Hetty's mental weakness.

Cooper employs the discrepancy between these two forms of naming to invalidate the prospect of self-determination. He observes that as the settlements expand, new names will replace those chosen by the Indians and trappers. As soon as the Glimmerglass is mapped, it will acquire a new title which Natty fears will be less "reasonable and resembling" (44). He mourns that change because white "christenings always foretell waste and destruction" (44). There is, Cooper implies, a bond between naming and destruction which transcends the inevitable process of wilderness clearing. The names the settlers have traditionally imposed on the forests are drawn from Europe. Whether those titles bear the prefix "new" or whether they honor a monarch or a military hero, they suggest the weight of history. His characters' surnames imply a similar burden. Natty and Chingachgook have earned wilderness titles, but they also have family names which restrict their freedom. Chingachgook is of the line of Uncas and is as a result bound by the demands of that heritage. Natty is limited by the imperatives of the Bumppo's. He cannot fully embrace the ways of his adopted tribe but must preserve the traditions of his race and family. Although he hopes to "live and die" with the Delawares, he must "strive to do a paleface's duty in a redskin society" (317). Judith's situation is even more difficult. Natty will not marry her because she is too highly

born; the officers of the garrison regard her "as the play-
thing of an idle hour rather than as an equal and a friend"
(170). She attempts to free herself from the limits of her
heritage by arguing that because her true father is unknown to her, she is "Judith and Judith only" (457). But
her declaration of independence is futile. Judith is, as her
duplication of her mother's fate implies, bound by her
nature.

Cooper undermines, then, the autonomy implicit in the
earned names of his characters. Like the identities children
assume in their games, those names are fictions which can
not withstand the force of reality. The violation of childish
fantasies is, in fact, the principal burden of *The Deerslayer*'s
narrative. The Glimmerglass is a world of play where pa-
rental authority evaporates and adult responsibilities are
suspended. Judith, as H. Daniel Peck observes, plays dress-
up in her mother's clothes, while Natty and Chingachgook
duel with what the Serpent calls a "child gun" (235).[19]
Cooper's evocation of the resonant memories of childhood
is masterful, and indeed, *The Deerslayer*'s power issues
primarily from that source. But Cooper does not abandon
himself or his readers to that reverie. The "child gun"
explodes in Natty's hand; Judith's gown does not convince
the Hurons that she is a woman of rank and authority.
When she enters their camp dressed in her mother's finery
and demands Natty's release, Rivenoak, the Huron chief,
smiles and says that "the Great Spirit sometimes puts very
bright clothes on very little animals" (557). Natty tells
her that her plan has failed because Rivenoak is an "on-
common man." So too is Cooper. In *The Deerslayer*, he
realizes the dream of his confident countrymen. He creates

19 Ibid., 69.

a character of heroic stature and a myth of eternal freedom and possibility. But then he withdraws that illusion, identifies it as a game of dress-up. He returns to the setting of *The Pioneers* and, in the mirror of the Glimmerglass, inverts the design of that novel. A myth disguised as history becomes history disguised as myth. The "newness" of the New World is the principal casualty of this transformation, but in that loss there is a gain. In denying American difference, Cooper diminishes our sense of election and leads us away from our city on a hill. The world beyond the Glimmerglass may be, as Judith fears, "full of misery," but it is a world and not an illusion.

Index

Adams, John Q., 126
Agamemnon (*Pioneers*), 19
American Democrat, The (1938), 37, 39
American Revolution, 9, 11, 71, 145
Ames, Fisher, 124–25
Anderson, Quentin, 175
Arrowhead (*Pathfinder*), 129–30, 135–36, 138, 140, 152
Associationist aesthetic, 20, 75–77

Ballston Spa, 70
Barthes, Roland, 159
Bat, Obed (*Prairie*): and the Enlightenment, 105; vs. Natty, 117–21
Beard, James Franklin, 36n, 107n
Bowley, Marius, 102n, 157n, 161, 173–74
Bicentennial, the, 43
Bold Dragoon, the, 20
Brackenridge, Hugh Henry, 21n, 96
Braddock, General, 53, 55, 130, 133
Bradford, William, 33
Brady, Charles A., 84n
Bryant, William Cullen, 76
Bumppo, Natty: abandons his station, 151–52; career of, 90–91; certain vision of, 55–56; courtship of, 141, 149–54; as cultural ideal, 181–82; death of,

103–4; dreams of, 153–54, 156; emotional appeal of, 29; as escapist figure, 174, 179–80; and human constancy, 118–21; vs. Hurry Harry, 161–64; imprisonment of, 24–25; vs. Ishmael Bush, 95, 113–15; vs. Judge Temple, 2, 16–17, 29; and Judith Hutter, 168, 170, 180, 182, 185–86; as "King of the Woods," 170–71; legendary status of, 147–49, 170–71; militant virtue of, 57; as model for Heyward, 56–57, 61–62, 67–71; as model for the actual, 174–75; vs. Obed Bat, 117–21; as precursor of Judge Temple, 24–25; reappearance in *Mohicans*, 47–48; and signs of nature, 60–61; singularity of, 56, 72, 74; as source of American identity, 9; transformation of, in *Prairie*, 100–104; uncoded vision of, 56; visits Chingachgook's grave, 30–31; vulnerability of, 152–54
Bush, Asa (*Prairie*), 110, 113
Bush, Esther (*Prairie*), 94, 96
Bush, Ishmael (*Prairie*): and justice, 113–15; and the law, 93–95; levels cottonwood grove, 94–95; as quintessential squatter, 92–96; and radical originality, 108–9; and repudia-

189